THE CIVIL WAR

THE
CIVIL
WAR

A CONCISE HISTORY

LOUIS P. MASUR

OXFORD
UNIVERSITY PRESS
2011

OXFORD
UNIVERSITY PRESS

Oxford University Press, Inc., publishes works that further
Oxford University's objective of excellence
in research, scholarship, and education.

Oxford   New York
Auckland   Cape Town   Dar es Salaam   Hong Kong   Karachi
Kuala Lumpur   Madrid   Melbourne   Mexico City   Nairobi
New Delhi   Shanghai   Taipei   Toronto

With offices in
Argentina   Austria   Brazil   Chile   Czech Republic   France   Greece
Guatemala   Hungary   Italy   Japan   Poland   Portugal   Singapore
South Korea   Switzerland   Thailand   Turkey   Ukraine   Vietnam

Published by Oxford University Press, Inc.
198 Madison Avenue, New York, NY 10016

www.oup.com

Oxford is a registered trademark of Oxford University Press

Library of Congress Cataloging-in-Publication Data
Masur, Louis P.
The Civil War : a concise history / Louis P. Masur.
p.   cm.
Includes bibliographical references and index.
ISBN 978-0-19-974048-2
1. United States—History—Civil War, 1861–1865.   I. Title.
E468.M155 2011
973.7—dc22
2010019460

3 5 7 9 8 6 4 2

Printed in the United States of America
on acid-free paper

For my teachers and my students

Human-nature will not change. In any future great national trial, compared with the men of this, we shall have as weak, and as strong; as silly and as wise; as bad and good. Let us, therefore, study the incidents of this, as philosophy to learn wisdom from, and none of them as wrongs to be revenged.

Abraham Lincoln, November 10, 1864

The Secession war? Nay, let me call it the Union war. Though whatever call'd, it is even yet too near us—too vast and too closely overshadowing—its branches unform'd yet, (but certain,) shooting too far into the future—and the most indicative and mightiest of them yet ungrown.

Walt Whitman, "Death of Abraham Lincoln," 1879

CONTENTS

On April 12, 1861, at around 4:30 in the morning, Confederate guns opened fire on Fort Sumter, situated in the harbor outside Charleston, South Carolina. A war began that lasted four years, claimed more than six hundred thousand lives, and forever transformed the nation.

The shooting may have started that day, but the conflict's origins came much earlier. Just when, of course, is impossible to say. Perhaps it was with the election of Abraham Lincoln, the first Republican president, a western lawyer and politician who came to office without any Southern support. Or perhaps it was with the bloodshed in Kansas in the mid-1850s, a rehearsal of sorts for the Civil War, which captured the nation's attention and reopened with a vengeance the thorny issue of slave expansion into the territories. Or back farther, to the Compromise of 1850, which settled little, or the Mexican War of 1846–48, or the fears and actions of abolitionists and slaveholders who parsed every event through a conspiratorial lens. Or farther still: the Nullification Crisis, Nat Turner's rebellion and the Virginia debate over abolishing slavery, or the Missouri Compromise. Looking back, some citizens contemplated the Constitution and blamed the framers for failing to resolve the tensions between state and nation, slavery and freedom. Sectional strain had all been building for a long time until, suddenly, the recurring threat of disunion became a stark reality.

Perhaps no event in American history has invited more speculation about whether it could have been avoided, or turned out differently, than the Civil War. It is an intriguing thought experiment to pose such questions as what if Lincoln had acquiesced on Southern secession, or what if a settlement guaranteeing slavery had been reached in the winter of

1860–61, or what if some general at any one of a half-dozen battles had managed to decimate the enemy army. But ultimately such "what if" questions tell us nothing about what was. As the narrator in Cormac McCarthy's novel *All the Pretty Horses* observes, "There is no one to tell us what might have been. We weep over the might have been, but there is no might have been. There never was."

This concise history seeks to explain what happened, how it transpired, and what it all meant. Causation is nearly as nettlesome a problem as contingency. In his masterpiece *War and Peace*, a draft of which he completed in 1863, Leo Tolstoy observed, "It is beyond the power of the human intellect to encompass all the causes of any phenomenon. But the impulse to search into causes is inherent in man's very nature." One can no more know what caused an event as complex as the Civil War than whether it could have been avoided. This is not to say key factors cannot be isolated: Slavery caused the Civil War, but in what ways? Disagreements over questions of sovereignty and Constitutional authority caused the Civil War, but how? Northerners and Southerners saw themselves as different, but why did those differences turn lethal and ultimately lead to horrific violence?

Despite these difficulties, it is important to sketch the contours of the war's origins, and I do so by surveying its long-term origins, short-term origins, and triggering events. The focus here is on states' rights and slavery and how the momentum of events led the nation to catastrophe. The story begins with the revolutionary era because the debates over the ratification of the Constitution, and the ways the delegates dealt with the issue of slavery, framed a disagreement that did not end. At times, the long lead-up to war may seem like a series of remotely connected acts, but these were more than prosaic events to be memorized only by schoolchildren. By 1860, decades of intensifying conflict over government authority with respect to the expansion of slavery swelled into the tsunami of secession.

The remainder of this volume is devoted to the war itself, its aims and methods, its costs and its results, its effects at home and abroad. Karl Marx and Frederick Engels observed from Europe in March 1862 that "from whatever standpoint one regards it, the American Civil War presents a spectacle without parallel in the annals of military history. The vast extent of the disputed territory; the far-flung front of the lines of operation; the numerical strength of the hostile armies, the creation of which hardly drew any support from a prior organizational basis; the fabulous cost of these armies; the manner of commanding them and the general tactical and strategic principles in accordance with which the war is being waged, are all new."[1]

Within a chronological narrative, I emphasize two central themes: for the Union, the war began as a limited war to restore the country, yet those aims shifted quickly, and the conflict ended as an all-out war of conquest that not only eradicated the Confederate government but fundamentally altered Southern society. Care must be taken, however, not to exaggerate the shift. From the start, the combat was never particularly restrained, but over time, as the depredations deepened, destruction not only of armies but also of citizens, cities, and landscapes became accepted, expanded, and codified as necessary acts of war. As early as August 1861, a few months into the war, one commentator predicted, "Our march will inevitably through the whole South be a trail of desolation."

He also predicted that "the only key to victory is a *Proclamation of Emancipation*." It took longer than many abolitionists and radical Republicans had hoped, but as part of the transformation of the war's purposes, the conflict became a war to abolish slavery. After January 1, 1863, the date of the Emancipation Proclamation, it was still unclear which side would emerge victorious in the war, but from then on it was certain that if the Union prevailed it would spell slavery's doom.[2]

This volume concludes with a consideration of the aftermath of April 9, 1865, the day General Lee met with General Grant and agreed to terms of surrender. While the military conflict largely ceased after that meeting at Appomattox Courthouse in Virginia, the war certainly was not finished. The clash over the policies of Reconstruction—also debated as restoration versus reformation (the labels themselves suggesting different approaches)—divided president and Congress, conservatives and radicals, Southerners and Northerners. When, and subject to what terms, would the rebel states resume their customary place in the nation? Would the country have the "new birth of freedom" that Lincoln had envisioned in his Gettysburg Address and what would that mean for the nearly four million African Americans?

By the time it was all over, the United States had been remade. In 1873, Mark Twain and Charles Dudley Warner, in their novel *The Gilded Age*, provided an epitaph for the era. They maintained that the Civil War and its immediate aftermath "uprooted institutions that were centuries old, changed the politics of a people, transformed the social life of half the country, and wrought so profoundly upon the entire national character that the influence cannot be measured short of two or three generations."[3] The occasion of the war's sesquicentennial is certainly an appropriate time again to take measure.

ACKNOWLEDGMENTS

I am grateful to my editor, Susan Ferber, for giving me an opportunity to write this book. She waited until I had completed two other projects, and I am thankful for her patience. Working with her has been a delight, and I am especially pleased again to be part of the Oxford list in American history. I offer my thanks as well to my agent, Zoe Pagnamenta, who continues to support my work.

I would like to thank my colleagues in the American Studies program at Trinity College: Davarian Baldwin, Scott Gac, Cheryl Greenberg, Christopher Hager, Joan Hedrick, Paul Lauter, Eugene Leach, Nancy Rossi, Scott Tang, Diana Paulin, and J. Ronald Spencer. Ron deserves special mention. Over a long career at Trinity, he has taught the Civil War era, and his knowledge is unparalleled. He is also a superb editor. Every page of this book has benefited from his keen editorial eye. I am indebted to him for his ongoing encouragement and friendship.

As always, my deepest thanks go to Bob Allison, Bill Decker, Jim Goodman, Doug Greenberg, Peter Mancall, Dave Masur, Mark Richman, Bruce Rossky, Aaron Sachs, and Tom Slaughter. For more than twenty years, Tom has read in draft nearly everything I have written, and the manuscript for this book is no exception. That he is starting to like my work concerns me.

My mother-in-law, Eileen Fox, passed away while this book was in press. I lost not only a loving, caring woman but also the best publicist one could hope for. The entire Fox family has always been supportive and proud of my work. I offer my deepest thanks to Ed, Amy, Robin, George, Laurie, Adam, Daniel, Murray, and Steven. I offer my appreciation as well to Deirdre and Jonathan Masur, and to Lois, David, Michael, and Betty Mallin, as well as Wally, Marlena, Larry, Dale, Jim, and Soni Masur. Confused by all the distinctions made by historians, my late parents, Seymour and Sarah Masur, simply told everyone I was a Civil War historian. Turns out, as with so many other things, they were right.

While this book is dedicated to all my teachers, there are several in particular I need to mention. At the Bronx High School of Science, Mr. Harrison and Mr. Seidenstein (as far as I am concerned they never had first names) first introduced me to the wonders of primary sources. At the University of Buffalo, Selig Adler, Edgar Dryden, Joe Fraden, Michael Frisch, Milton Plesur, and William Sylvester exposed me to the challenges and joys of history and literature. But no one was more important than Dave Gerber, who invited a timid sophomore to lunch one day and as a result changed my life. Dave encouraged me to apply to graduate school, and he has remained a mentor and friend for more than thirty years.

At Princeton University, it was my great, good luck to have had my first research seminar with Jim McPherson. I became hooked on the nineteenth century and, over the years in graduate school, I had an opportunity to serve as Jim's research assistant, precept for his Civil War class, and visit Gettysburg Battlefield with him and our students. Jim also generously read a draft of the manuscript for this volume and saved me from numerous errors. I am especially indebted to Dan Rodgers for always pushing me to think and write more critically and clearly, and also to Stan Katz, John Murrin, and Jim Oakes for their support.

This book is also dedicated to my students, from whom I have learned so much, whether at Princeton, the University of California at Riverside, Harvard University, the City College of New York, or, since 2004, Trinity College. Special mention must be made of the following members of the class of 2010: Kate Goodman, Grace Green, Lily Haskins, Rebecca Herrigel, Catherine Shortliffe, and Sophia Alyssa Simpson. I owe a special thanks to Mike Klein and Jim Petrucci, two of my first students, circa 1984, and now good friends.

Jani, Ben, and Sophie: our wild, real love never lets me down.

THE CIVIL WAR

CHAPTER 1

THE ORIGINS OF THE CIVIL WAR

SOUTHERNERS WHO SUPPORTED SECESSION FELT THAT THEY
had no choice. They had tried, for more than fifty years, to make a go of
the experiment in national government, but as they had feared from the
start, centralized authority threatened to sweep aside local control; the
federal government seemed to trample on the sovereignty of state governments. When South Carolinians seceded on December 20, 1860, they
saw themselves as upholding the principle on which the American
Revolution had first been fought: opposition to remote, tyrannical
authority. The *Charleston Mercury* declared: "The tea has been thrown
overboard; the revolution of 1860 has been initiated." Mississippi issued
a declaration of the immediate causes for secession that listed, on the
model of the Declaration of Independence, Mississipians' grievances
against a government that was perceived as consistently hostile to slavery.
"For far less cause than this," the document concluded, "our Fathers separated from the Crown of England."[1]

LONG-TERM ORIGINS

The colonies may have banded together in 1776 for the purpose of separation from England, but they had as little affection for one another as
for central government. These antagonisms divided them not simply between North and South, but between state and state and between region
and region, as those in New York disdained the residents of Connecticut

and those along Virginia's coast often battled the settlers along the state's western frontier. The first governmental structure created by the American patriots, the Articles of Confederation, allotted so little power to the new central government that it could do almost nothing unless all the states agreed. Article 2 read: "Each state retains its sovereignty, freedom, and independence, and every power, jurisdiction, and right, which is not, by this Confederation, expressly delegated to the United States."

By 1787, it had become clear to many political leaders that the Articles of Confederation were not working. Under these terms, Congress could not collect taxes or regulate trade. Dismay over unjust taxation had been the pivotal issue that led to the Revolution, and in the early republic it was again controversial, only this time the conflict was replayed within states. For example, in Massachusetts, residents in the western part of the state rebelled against actions taken by the state government, led by Governor John Hancock, in the eastern part. Known as Shays' Rebellion, the insurrection was only one of several that would play out along the east-west, seaport-frontier axis in the late eighteenth century. With the ratification of the Constitution of the United States, those east-west tensions would gradually rotate in a north-south direction.

The Constitution created a tripartite form of government that sought to check and balance the powers of each branch, all the while giving the federal government power it had not previously held, most notably over taxes and interstate commerce. The fifty-five men who gathered in Philadelphia in the summer of 1787 and framed the new constitution worried about the nation's survival, as well as their own economic interests, and the document they sent forward for ratification sought to compromise on a number of issues, not the least being slavery.

The institution is referred to explicitly three times in the document, but the word "slave" never appears. Article 1, section 2, describing how representatives would be apportioned, mentions "three-fifths of all other persons." Article 1, section 9, states that the importation of "such persons as any of the states now existing should think proper to admit" would not be prohibited prior to 1808. And article 4, section 2, asserts that no person "held to service or labour in one state, under the laws thereof, escaping into another" can be "discharged" from such labor by the laws of the latter.

A different document adopted by the Confederation Congress that year displayed fewer qualms about the word. The Northwest Ordinance of 1787 opened up the territory north of the Ohio River and east of the Mississippi to settlement by U.S. citizens. Article 6 said "there shall be neither slavery nor involuntary servitude in the said territory." When Mississippi issued its causes of secession, the first item on its list was the "hostility" to the institution of slavery evidenced in the Northwest Ordinance.

For the most part, the hostility evinced toward slavery by the founders was latent rather than manifest. To be sure, in the wake of the Revolution, Northern states adopted gradual emancipation plans: Pennsylvania in 1780, Connecticut and Rhode Island in 1784, New York in 1799, and New Jersey in 1804. The Massachusetts state constitution declared in 1780: "all men are born free and equal." And a swelling chorus of jurists, legislators, and the enslaved themselves began to highlight the paradox of slavery in a land dedicated to liberty. Massachusetts justice William Cushing insisted that "the idea of slavery is inconsistent with our conduct and Constitution." Oliver Ellsworth of Connecticut, a signer of the U.S. Constitution, proclaimed "slavery in time will not be a speck in our Country." Even before Jefferson penned the Declaration of Independence, a group of slaves in Boston had declared in a petition to the governor and general court that "we have in common with all other men a naturel [sic] right to our freedoms without Being depriv'd of them by our fellow men."[2]

Thomas Jefferson, one of many slaveholding founders, struggled at times over what to do about the institution. He knew it was engrained in the Southern economy and way of life, and he believed that blacks were innately inferior to whites ("the difference is fixed in nature," he would write). At the same time, he despaired over the "boisterous passions" and "unremitting despotism" embedded in the relationship between master and slave. "I tremble for my country," he confessed, "when I reflect that God is just: that his justice cannot sleep forever."[3]

Jefferson, along with many others, also trembled over the new powers vested in the federal government by the proposed Constitution of the United States. Writing to James Madison, who played a prominent role at the Constitutional Convention, Jefferson insisted that a bill of rights be added: it "is what the people are entitled to against every government on earth." Nothing would mollify other opponents to the Constitution. Factions in every state opposed it for a variety of specific reasons, all of them rooted in an abiding aversion to relinquishing local control to a national entity. Supporting ratification were the Federalists, as they came to call themselves, in a clever appropriation of language—"federal" had always indicated state or local. Anti-Federalists opposed it. This was true both north and south. In Massachusetts, the vote for ratification went 187–168; in Virginia, it went 89–78.[4]

In opposing ratification, no less a figure than Patrick Henry, governor of Virginia and a leading revolutionary who had once declared "Give me liberty or give me death," expressed the fear that the new, more powerful government might one day interfere with slavery. Henry asked why a clause was "omitted to secure us that property in slaves which we held now." He feared its omission was done by design. The government might lay such heavy taxes on slaves as to compel emancipation; and then "the Southern States would be the only sufferers." Congress had been given power over taxation. Who was to say that the power wouldn't one day be used explicitly against Virginia's interests? Henry said he had "smelled a rat" and stayed away from the convention in the summer of 1787. Although the Anti-Federalists did not manage to defeat ratification, they made certain that a bill of rights was included. The Constitution says "we the people of the United States," but not everyone felt fully invested in the enterprise.[5]

In the late eighteenth century, when Americans spoke of their country they still meant their state, not the nation. Almost no one thought of the United States as anything but plural, and straightaway a tradition emerged of challenging the authority of the national government at every turn. When the Federalists, the political party that emerged out of advocacy for ratification of the Constitution, held power, they were opposed by the Democratic-Republicans, many of them former Anti-Federalists. In 1798, the Federalists passed the Alien and Sedition Acts, designed to exert control over dissidents and stifle the expression of political opposition. In response, Virginia and Kentucky passed resolutions denying that Congress had the authority to deport aliens or prosecute for seditious libel. James Madison and Thomas Jefferson wrote the resolves, which also articulated a compact theory of government: that the national government existed only as a compact or agreement that the states could break if they so desired. The Virginia resolution offered "warm attachment to the union of the states" but made it clear that it viewed the "powers of the federal government as resulting from the compact to which the states are parties." The resolution went on to state that "in case of a deliberate, palpable, and dangerous exercise of other powers, not granted by the said compact, the states who are parties thereto, have the right, and are in duty bound, to interpose for arresting the progress of the evil, and for maintaining within their respective limits, the authorities, rights and liberties appertaining to them."[6]

The doctrine of state interposition, or nullification, would one day lead the nation toward civil war. But at the time its toxicity was not understood. Soon enough, Jefferson came into office, the Democratic-Republicans repealed the Alien and Sedition Acts, and it seemed that politics would defuse future threats. Quite often, whenever states or regions disagreed with a policy they threatened to interpose or nullify it, or even secede from the union. In 1814–15, a group of New England Federalists, dismayed by Jefferson's and Madison's policies, especially the purchase of Louisiana Territory and the embargo during the ongoing War of 1812, threatened to establish a New England confederacy. The final report that emanated from a convention in Hartford suggested that "if the union be destined to dissolution" then perhaps "some new form of confederacy" could be established. The Federalists didn't get very far, and with victory in the War of 1812 and a new nationalist tide surging, they would soon be extinct as a political party.[7]

Within a few years of the Hartford Convention, the nation's attention would turn to another region and constitutional questions of nation versus state would be tethered to the issue of antislavery versus slavery. In 1819, the residents of Missouri sought to draft a state constitution and seek admission to the nation, which at the time, had a balanced number of slave and free states (eleven of each). A proposed resolution to restrict any additional slaves from entering the territory set off legislative fireworks as politicians debated the constitutionality of Congress prohibiting slavery. The crisis resolved when Maine also applied for statehood: in what became known as the Missouri Compromise, Congress admitted the two states simultaneously, one slave and the other free. Added to the bill was an amendment that forever excluded slavery from the remainder of the Louisiana Territory north of the latitude of 36°30'. The Senate vote on the bill was almost entirely sectional, the South voting in favor and the North voting against.

In the spring of 1820, Thomas Jefferson followed national events from Monticello, and he expressed his fears in letters to friends: the Missouri question, he told one correspondent, "like a fire-bell in the night awakened and filled me with terror. I considered it at once as the knell of the union...a geographical line, coinciding with a marked principle, moral and political, once conceived and held up to the angry passions of men, will never be obliterated; and every new irritation will mark it deeper and deeper." To another he wrote: "I have been among the most sanguine in believing that our Union would be of long duration. I now doubt it much."[8]

At the time the Missouri crisis erupted, statesmen were also considering the place of blacks on American soil. In 1816, the formation of the American Colonization Society gave organizational form to the belief that blacks would be better off settled in colonies back in Africa. Men including Thomas Jefferson, James Monroe, Henry Clay, Daniel Webster, and John Randolph supported the society's goals. Abraham Lincoln would as well. They did so out of a belief that the prejudice of race was so strong in America that free blacks would never successfully integrate into society, and that slavery itself was a "necessary evil" that warped Southern institutions and might best be abolished gradually.

Most free blacks, who numbered more than three hundred thousand in 1830, opposed colonization. They proclaimed America their country and asserted their rights as citizens. "See your Declaration Americans," advised David Walker, a free black living in Boston, reminding readers of the injunction "all men are created equal." In his *Appeal to the Colored Citizens of the World*, Walker not only condemned colonization of free blacks, he also advocated slave rebellion as the road to freedom. Even William Lloyd Garrison, the fiery abolitionist who initially favored colonization and then begged forgiveness from the public for his earlier support of the doctrine, and who would inaugurate a new assault on slavery that would lead Southerners to put a price on his head, deprecated the "spirit and tendency of this Appeal."[9]

On January 1, 1831, Garrison launched the *Liberator*, a weekly newspaper that transformed the rhetoric of abolition. No longer was any form of gradual emancipation acceptable. Now, he called for immediate abolition. Fired by a religious vision of the nation washing its hands of the sin of slavery, and wedded to a literal reading of the Declaration of Independence, Garrison denounced slaveholders as barbaric and inhumane and vowed to press the issue with all his energy. "I shall be harsh as truth and as uncompromising as justice," he said, and he meant it. In time he would denounce the Constitution as a "covenant with death and an agreement with hell."

When later that year the Virginia slave Nat Turner led a rebellion in Southampton County that slaughtered some sixty whites, terrified Southerners blamed Garrison for inciting the slaves to revolt and lamented the lack of a law to punish the resident of one state for inciting insurrection in another. Although Turner, who saw himself as a prophet and took an eclipse of the sun as a sign to proceed, had acted independently, his capture and execution did little to ease the anxieties of slaveholders who had convinced themselves that slaves were happy, docile, and content. It now required additional effort to sustain that delusion.

In an extraordinary moment, led by Thomas Jefferson Randolph, the Virginia legislature debated the gradual abolition of slavery in the state. Although some legislators proclaimed that "it is an act of injustice, tyranny, and oppression to hold any part of the human race in bondage against their consent," many more defended slavery and denounced schemes of abolition that entailed additional taxes to fund the removal of all free blacks from the state. In the end, Virginia rejected abolition and instead refortified its black codes and took measures to prevent future insurrections. But Randolph, Thomas Jefferson's grandson, looked into the future and saw in it the inevitability of the dissolution of the Union and a violent war between North and South.

Unlike Randolph, most Virginians quickly rationalized Turner's rebellion as an aberration. One legislator proclaimed that the slaves "are as happy a laboring class as exists upon the habitable globe...contented, peaceful, and harmless." Indeed, just as a new abolitionist ideology had taken root in the North, so too did Southerners now articulate a new proslavery ideology. No longer was the institution seen as a necessary evil. Now, many Southern statesmen averred, it was a positive good.[10]

No one expressed the position more explicitly than John C. Calhoun, senator from South Carolina, who had served as vice president under John Quincy Adams and Andrew Jackson. "Instead of evil," Calhoun declared, slavery was a "positive good...the most solid and durable foundation on which to rear free and stable political institutions." It was free laborers rather than slaves who were exploited. Masters, Calhoun believed, formed a paternalistic relation to their bondsmen, and Southern society in general exhibited greater honor and civility than any part of the North. A racial ideology built around white supremacy united slaveholders and nonslaveholders and provided Southern states with a common identity.[11]

Calhoun spoke for a Southern aristocracy that was reaping untold wealth from the production of cotton for export. Indeed, the ideology of slavery as a positive good followed the expansion of cotton production that soared with the invention of the cotton gin. By 1860, the region grew nearly three-fourths of the world's supply. And the cotton trade also enriched the Midwest, which sold food supplies to the South, and the Northeast, where cotton textile mills were booming. In 1858, Senator James Henry Hammond of South Carolina spoke confidently of the place of Southern cotton in the world economy. "You dare not make war on cotton," he threatened. "No power on earth dares to make war upon it. Cotton is king."[12]

An early test of the South's economic power, and the constitutionality of nullification, came in 1832 when a South Carolina convention, infuriated by the high import duties set by the tariff of 1828, adopted an Ordinance of Nullification. Calhoun was the leading exponent of the view that the Union was a voluntary compact among sovereign states, and he had published anonymously a pamphlet titled *Exposition and Protest* that made the case for the unconstitutionality of the tariff of 1828.

Calhoun argued that Congress did not have the authority to pass protective tariffs, that such tariffs benefited Northern industry at the expense of Southern agriculture, and that if the central government had the power to impose tariffs, it also had the power to attack slavery. The only check on the power of the majority, Calhoun asserted, was "the constitutional right of the States to interpose in order to protect their powers." As noted, "interposition" was another word for "nullification." Alexis de Tocqueville, visiting America, observed that "the Union has never shown so much weakness as on the celebrated question of the tariff." John Quincy Adams saw nullification "in no other light than as *organized civil War*."[13]

Other Southern states did not follow the lead of the Carolinians on nullification, and the Democratic, slaveholding Southern president Andrew Jackson made it clear where he stood on the issue: "disunion by armed force is *treason*." A quiet compromise on tariff rates and the threat of federal military action led South Carolina to repeal its nullification ordinance. But the idea of the Union as a compact in which the states were sovereign and had the right to nullify what they considered unauthorized acts by the federal government had been fully aired.[14]

SHORT-TERM ORIGINS

The core questions of slavery and government power continued to pulsate, but so, too, did many other issues. The 1830s and 1840s brought religious revivalism and economic transformation—manufacturing and industry developed at an unprecedented rate in the North. The Southern economy also grew, though it remained overwhelmingly agricultural. Immigration swelled the Northern population, and improvements in transportation—steamboats, canals, railroads—opened up the interior for trade and settlement. From 1840 to 1850, the population of the United States increased from seventeen to twenty-three million. There were more than three million slaves, half a million more than ten years earlier.

The North and the South tend to be treated as monoliths, but within these sections there were great variations. The North included cities on the seacoast but also mill towns and farming communities inland; it incorporated the regional differences among New England, the Mid-Atlantic, and the Midwest. Northern occupational structure included wage laborers, farmers, skilled tradesmen, professionals, and myriad others. Economic inequality had continued to increase in the decades since the revolution, but a belief that anyone could succeed governed the era, and people were in constant motion seeking their best opportunities.

White Southerners also exhibited mobility, pushing west both with and without slaves. They, too, sought prosperity. In 1860, about one-quarter of Southern families owned slaves, and more than half of those who did possessed fewer than five. The members of the planter elite owned twenty or more slaves, and while they accounted for just 3 percent of all white families, they exercised disproportionate political power and among themselves owned more than half of all slaves. The Deep South, which produced most of the cotton, differed from the Upper South, but white Southerners shared a common identity centered on such values as public honor and kin loyalty, not to mention racial superiority. Two-thirds of Southerners were nonslaveholding farmers—yeomen—but they identified their interests, as well as their dreams of upward mobility, with the slaveholding elite.

The two main political parties, Whigs and Democrats, differed on a number of central issues. Although the Whigs managed to win the presidency only twice, they appealed to many forward-looking voters with their "American System": a program of government-aided economic development that stressed investing in manufacturing, supporting tariffs, favoring a national bank, developing internal improvements such as canals, roads, and turnpikes, and favoring moral reforms such as temperance. The Democrats championed strictly limited government, opposing any national policy that threatened local control or the individual liberty of whites. If the Whigs tended toward antislavery, the Democrats' emphasis on states' rights and their advocacy of territorial expansion gave the party a proslavery cast that ensured it broad popularity in the South. While professing support for laborers, small farmers, and immigrants, the Democratic Party also evinced intense hostility toward free blacks and avoided saying or doing anything slaveholders would find objectionable. As long as a Democrat held the presidency, slavery would be safe politically.

An example of Southern Democratic influence can be seen in the imposition of a "gag rule" in Congress that banned discussion of antislavery petitions and led some Northerners to wonder about what other freedoms the slave power—the Southern slaveholding political elite—might eliminate. In 1840, political abolitionists formed the Liberty Party, which ran on a platform of immediate emancipation, but the party attracted few voters. By arousing the explosive issue of whether slavery would be allowed to expand into new areas, the annexation of Texas in 1845 and the war with Mexico from 1846 to 1848 initiated a train of events that ultimately led to the Civil War. The issues of slavery, states' rights, and territorial expansion combined to shear the nation apart.

The United States started huge, and would grow even larger. The Louisiana Purchase in 1803 doubled the size of the nation, and the desire for territory remained insatiable. Many Americans embraced the doctrine of "manifest destiny," the belief that it was America's providential mission to spread across the continent. Overland journeys took Americans to all parts of the continent, but no destination had attracted more settlers than Texas. In 1836, the Texans declared independence from Mexico, and in 1845 the area was annexed and admitted to statehood over the bitter opposition of those who vehemently resisted the addition of another slave state. In short order, James Polk sent troops to Texas to defend a border that Mexico claimed belonged to a Mexican territory whose independence from Mexico they did not recognize in the first place.

The United States declared war on May 13, 1846. When it ended nearly two years later, Mexico not only ceded all claims to Texas above the Rio Grande boundary, it also surrendered California and New Mexico, a large Mexican province. Critics saw the war as an exercise in military conquest and territorial aggrandizement. Ralph Waldo Emerson, a founder of transcendentalism and a popular public lecturer, predicted that "the United States will conquer Mexico, but it will be as the man swallows the arsenic, which brings him down in turn. Mexico will poison us."[15]

Within three months of the war's outbreak, the issue of slavery in the territories became politicized in ways it had not been since the Missouri crisis a quarter century earlier. This time, there would be no workable compromise. At one extreme, David Wilmot, an obscure Pennsylvania congressman, introduced a proviso that would prohibit slavery in any territory acquired from Mexico. At the other extreme, Calhoun argued that Congress had no power to prevent citizens from bringing their property, including slaves, into the new territories, which, he argued, were the common possession of the states alone, not of any sovereign federal government. Seeking a middle way, Northern Democrats developed the doctrine of popular sovereignty, which would leave it to the residents of each territory to decide the issue for themselves. It sounded good, democratic, and fair. But popular sovereignty obscured more than it clarified. When would territories decide on their status as slave or free—when the territory was first organized or not until it had sufficient population to draw up a constitution and apply for statehood? Perhaps a simpler solution existed, thought some: extend to the Pacific the Missouri Compromise boundary between slave and free territories at the 36°30' line.

Fearful that Congress would ban slavery in the new territories, nine slaveholding states sent delegates to a convention in Nashville in June 1850 to discuss defensive measures to be taken. Talk of secession filled the air. Langdon Cheves of South Carolina, a former congressman who was born in 1776, encouraged these states to "unite and you shall form one of the most splendid empires on which the sun ever shone." But on this occasion, the moderates won out and supported compromise.[16]

The separate legislative bills that would be referred to as the Compromise of 1850 constituted the final political act in the careers of Whig leader Henry Clay, John Calhoun, and Daniel Webster, the Massachusetts senator who had once declared "liberty and union, now and forever, one and inseparable," and now supported compromise with slaveholders by saying he was not a Northern man but an American.

The compromise admitted California as the sixteenth free state, upsetting the balance between slave and free states. Calhoun, too ill to deliver his own speech, listened as another senator read his words: he warned that the act would destroy "irretrievably the equilibrium between the two sections." In a concession to slaveholders, a new Fugitive Slave Act was adopted that provided for federal officials to pursue and return to captivity enslaved people who escaped to free states. A third bill abolished the slave trade in Washington, D.C. Two other bills organized Utah and New Mexico territories, with the status of slavery there to be decided under the doctrine of popular sovereignty. A final measure settled a festering dispute over the Texas–New Mexico boundary.

Within two years, Clay was dead. Abraham Lincoln, who greatly admired the statesman, delivered a eulogy at the statehouse in Springfield, Illinois. He acknowledged the fact of Clay's slaveholding, but added "he ever was, on principle and in feeling, opposed to slavery." But Clay had not believed "it could be at *once* eradicated, without producing a greater evil, even to the cause of human liberty itself." Lincoln denounced both extremes on the issue of slavery: "those who would shiver into fragments the Union of these States...rather than slavery should continue a single hour," as well as those at the opposite extreme who "for the sake of perpetuating slavery, are beginning to assail and to ridicule the white-man's charter of freedom, the declaration that 'all men are created free and equal.'" Lincoln admired Clay's middle position, but that position was no longer viable and, in time, Lincoln himself would have to move to one end of the spectrum or the other.[17]

The competing ideas of slavery as beneficial versus slavery as evil were represented in numerous broadsides and cartoons that offered a potent visual rhetoric easily grasped by all members of the public. These images relied on caricature and drama and helped shape the ways Americans thought about the crisis over slavery. For example, in 1850, a print titled *Slavery as it Exists in America. Slavery as it Exists in England* compared slave labor with free labor to the advantage of the former. The top panel shows happy-go-lucky slaves dancing and singing. In the background two visiting Northerners discuss the institution with two slaveholders. "Is it possible that we of the North have been so deceived by false reports?" asks one. The bottom panel depicts a scene in a British textile factory where the workers are ragged and emaciated. A mother exclaims, "Oh dear! What wretched slaves this Factory life makes me and my children."

Slavery as it Exists in America. Slavery as it Exists in England (Boston, 1850). Courtesy of Library of Congress.

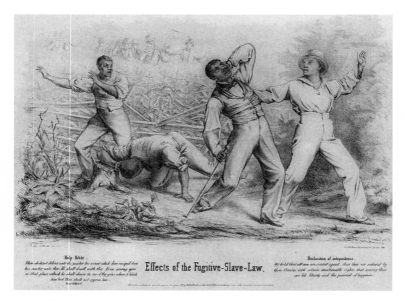

Effects of the Fugitive-Slave-Law (New York, 1850). Courtesy of Library of Congress.

By comparison, that same year a New York publisher issued a lithograph titled *Effects of the Fugitive-Slave-Law*. Appearing less than a month after passage of the Fugitive Slave Act, the print shows four well-dressed black men shot down in a cornfield. Texts from the Bible and the Declaration of Independence adorn the bottom of the print. The effects of the Fugitive Slave Act, suggests the image, will be the routine murder of black men, whether slave or free, in violation of all humanity.

For Northerners, the movement against slavery took a dramatic turn in 1852 with the publication of Harriet Beecher Stowe's novel *Uncle Tom's Cabin*. The book was a sensation, selling more copies than any other work except the Bible. A decade later, when Lincoln met the diminutive Stowe, he supposedly said, "so you're the little lady who started the big war." The story is almost certainly apocryphal, but *Uncle Tom's Cabin* did what few other works had managed to accomplish: in its depiction of the lives and struggles of slaves and their masters, it made slavery the central moral dilemma of the age for white, Northern Christian women whose hearts were sundered by the stories of Eliza, and Tom, and Little Eva. Southerners denounced the novel as utterly false in its depiction of slave life and banned it from the region.

If slaveholders perceived the existence of a Northern conspiracy to eradicate slavery, Northerners believed there was a slave power conspiracy to extend the institution. In 1854, Bostonians stood helpless as federal agents captured runaway slave Anthony Burns and marched him to the dock, where a boat waited to carry him back to his master. Burns's freedom was eventually purchased, but Southerners had made their point: under the terms of the Fugitive Slave Act, the federal government was committed to protecting the property rights of slaveholders.

That same year, antislavery and proslavery forces set on a collision course when the Kansas-Nebraska crisis erupted. Senator Stephen Douglas, Democrat from Illinois, who had played a critical role in the Compromise of 1850, proposed a bill organizing the territory west of Missouri as Kansas and west of Iowa and Minnesota as Nebraska—the Kansas-Nebraska Act. The Act provided that popular sovereignty would govern the issue of slavery in the territories and, in a bombshell that had the effect of unifying antislavery forces, included an amendment in effect repealing the Missouri Compromise, which had excluded slavery north of the 36°30' line.

Countless Northerners saw the Act as a "gross violation of a sacred pledge" made by Congress to keep slavery contained geographically, and as part of a plot by Southern proslavery forces. Whatever Douglas's political ambitions, he became a pariah in parts of the country. Primarily because of the passage of the Act, the political party system underwent fundamental realignment. The Whig Party, which had emerged after the disintegration of the Federalists, collapsed. In its place rose the Republican Party, created out of different constituencies—Northern Whigs, Democrats, Free-Soilers, Know-Nothings, who favored native-born Americans over immigrants, and an array of other antislavery elements. The Republicans became the party of antislavery, Protestant capitalism and, even more important for the fate of the nation, existed as a strictly sectional party. There had been Southern Whigs and Northern Whigs, but there were virtually no Southern Republicans. Northern Democrats paid a price for the Kansas-Nebraska Act, losing sixty-six of ninety-one free-state seats in the congressional elections of 1854 and

1855. No longer could the political party system serve to balance sectional interests and excitations.[18]

Lincoln used the occasion of the Kansas-Nebraska crisis to reemerge from political retirement. He had left Congress after one term in March 1849 to return to the practice of law. Speaking at Peoria, Illinois, he denounced the Act as "wrong in its direct effect, letting slavery into Kansas and Nebraska—and wrong in its prospective principle, allowing it to spread to every other part of the wide world, where men can be found inclined to take it." In the speech, Lincoln provided a précis of the problem before the nation: how to deal with "the monstrous injustice of slavery." He did not blame Southerners, and admitted that if he had all the power in the world he would not know what to do about the institution. But he could not tolerate the new defense of slavery as "a moral right." He wanted to return to the revolutionary generation's understanding, allowing it to exist as legal right and necessity and nothing more. And he wanted to prevent the spread of slavery beyond the fifteen states where it existed.[19]

But it was not possible to restore the equilibrium of 1776. Too much had changed, too many events had intervened. How far the nation's leaders had fallen from the founders became evident to Northerners when on May 22, 1856, Representative Preston Brooks of South Carolina viciously caned Senator Charles Sumner of Massachusetts as he sat at his desk in the Senate chamber. Brooks was avenging the honor of his cousin, whom Sumner had denounced in a speech several days earlier. Southerners saw the caning as an act of honor and justice; Northerners saw it as a symbol of the savage violence of a Southern region that would do anything to defend, even nationalize, slavery.

Sumner was not the only one bleeding; indeed his caning came the day after a destructive proslavery raid on Lawrence, Kansas. In 1856 Kansas became a battleground, a rehearsal of sorts for the Civil War. The territory erupted in violence as proslavery Missourians and antislavery midwesterners raced to the region to form territorial governments. Competing governments emerged, a proslavery one at Lecompton, the result of a fraudulent election, and an antislavery one at Topeka that was extralegal. After the assault on Lawrence and the beating of Sumner, John Brown, a wild-eyed New Englander who had come with his sons to Kansas in 1855, took revenge by killing a father, his two sons, and two other men at Pottawatomie Creek. Guerilla warfare between border ruffians and Free-Soiler fighters became the norm. Kansas had become "Bleeding Kansas," and the nation followed events with growing anxiety.

Clearly, the political system was breaking down, unable to contain sectional rivalry and violence. Perhaps, thought Chief Justice Roger Taney, the Supreme Court could resolve once and for all the nation's split over slavery. On March 6, 1857, in *Dred Scott v. Sandford*, a divided Supreme Court ruled on the case of a slave who argued that his residence in Illinois and the Wisconsin territory had freed him from bondage. The majority ruled that Scott remained a slave, that as a slave he was not a citizen and had "no rights which the white man was bound to respect," and that the Missouri Compromise ban on slavery was unconstitutional because it deprived citizens of their property without due process of law.

Taney's decision did not have the effect he imagined. Southern slaveholders may have applauded it, but outside of the South the decision energized the Republican Party and confirmed the worst fears of Northerners who perceived a slave power conspiracy afoot in America. It was Northerners now who spoke of defying an arm of the federal government: the *New York Independent* declared, "The Decision of the Supreme Court is the Moral Assassination of a Race and Cannot be Obeyed." Lincoln put the case most directly in a speech at Springfield the following year: "we shall *lie down* pleasantly dreaming that the people of *Missouri* are on the verge of making their State *free*, and we shall *awake* to the *reality*, instead, that the *Supreme* Court has made *Illinois* a *slave* State."[20]

In the same speech, Lincoln uttered fateful words. Quoting the biblical injunction "A house divided against itself cannot stand," Lincoln said, "I believe this government cannot endure, permanently half *slave* and half *free*. I do not expect the Union to be *dissolved*—I do not expect the house to *fall*—but I *do* expect it will cease to be divided. It will become *all* one thing, or *all* the other."

TRIGGERS

In many ways, white Southerners had good reason in the fall of 1859 to feel that slavery was secure from government interference and that they could continue to be part of the nation while keeping a commitment to their sense of region and rights. After all, the president, James Buchanan, was a Democrat from Pennsylvania who owed his election to the South.

The Supreme Court clearly supported the rights of slaveholders. Democrats controlled Congress. And while the Democratic Party suffered in the free states because of the Southern attempt, backed by the president, to make Kansas a slave state under the fraudulent Lecompton constitution, some Democrats took pleasure, no doubt, in Stephen Douglas defeating Abraham Lincoln in the Illinois senate race in 1858. There was little reason not to believe that with general prosperity returning following a financial panic in 1857, the future of the nation, despite the bitterness over the issues of slavery in the territories and slavery as a moral question, looked bright.

And then, on October 16, 1859, John Brown led an assault on the federal arsenal, then in Harper's Ferry, Virginia. His plan was to confiscate the arms stored there and distribute them to the slaves, who he believed would embrace his effort to create a mass insurrection. Brown's attack party included five black men and had the secret support of six influential New Englanders who agreed to fund his fight. Soon enough, the marines, under command of Robert E. Lee, arrived, stormed the arsenal, and captured Brown. Perhaps if Brown had been killed by the officer who led the charge and stabbed the leader with what turned out to be his ceremonial dress sword, not his saber, what followed might not have had the impact it did.

Brown was tried, convicted of treason, and sentenced to hang. He became a martyr to the abolitionist cause, a wild prophet who proclaimed that "the crimes of this guilty land will never be purged away but with blood." That was ominous enough for Southern slaveholders. Even worse was the empathy and support Brown received from many Northerners who came close to sanctifying him. Emerson predicted he would make "the gallows as glorious as the cross."[21]

Southerners, proud of their region, steeped in honor, devoted to their way of life, and determined to maintain white supremacy, could not tolerate what they considered Brown's abominable act and Northern support of it. They now viewed any form of opposition to slavery as tantamount to agitation for armed insurrection. After the invasion, reported Richmond's newspapers, "thousands of men...who, a month ago, scoffed at the idea of dissolution of the Union...now hold the opinion that its days are numbered."[22]

The election of 1860 proved decisive. Lincoln carried all free states except New Jersey, which he split with Stephen Douglas, the candidate of

Northern Democrats, who also won Missouri. Vice President John Breckinridge of Kentucky was the candidate of Southern Democrats and took eleven slave states. John Bell, of the newly formed Constitutional Union Party, carried Virginia, Kentucky, and Tennessee, his home state. Lincoln was on the ballot in only five Southern states. He took less than 40 percent of the overall popular vote, but he won 180 electoral votes, 28 more than were needed for victory.

The election of Lincoln, who like other Republicans was devoted to the ideal of free labor and condemned slavery as a moral, social, and political evil, gave the South's extreme proslavery "fire-eaters" their long-sought opportunity to lead their states out of the Union. An Atlanta newspaper declared, "let the consequences be what they may—whether the Potomac is crimsoned in human gore, and Pennsylvania Avenue is paved ten fathoms in depth with mangled bodies, or whether the last vestige of liberty is swept from the face of the American continent, the South will never submit to such humiliation and degradation as the inauguration of Abraham Lincoln."[23]

South Carolina seceded from the United States on December 20, 1860. Two days later, Lincoln wrote to Alexander Stephens, a longtime congressman from Georgia and a former Whig, and asked, "Do the people of the South really entertain fears that a Republican administration would, *directly*, or *indirectly*, interfere with their slaves, or with them, about their slaves?" Lincoln sought through Stephens to reassure the South that "there is no cause for such fears."[24]

In the same letter, Lincoln put the causes of secession in axiomatic terms: "you think slavery is *right* and ought to be extended; while we think it is *wrong* and ought to be restricted. That I suppose is the rub." William Henry Seward, the antislavery senator from New York who would serve as Lincoln's secretary of state, had put the matter more directly in 1858 by declaring the North-South struggle "an irrepressible conflict between opposing and enduring forces, and it means the United States must and will, sooner or later, become either entirely a slaveholding nation, or entirely a free-labor nation." Lincoln could reassure secessionists all he wanted that he would not interfere with slavery, but they had not forgotten his earlier public statements about containing slavery and placing it "in the course of ultimate extinction."[25]

With the New Year, Mississippi, Florida, Alabama, Georgia, Louisiana, and Texas followed South Carolina's lead and seceded from the Union.

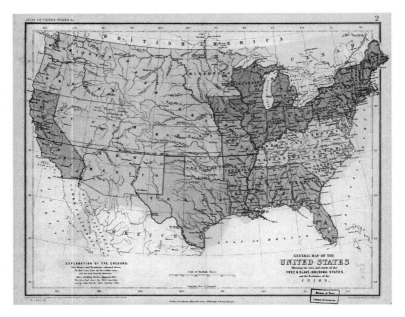

General Map of the United States Showing the Area and Extent of the Free and
Slave-holding States (Edinburgh, 1857). Courtesy of Library of Congress.

Any map clearly showed how much slave territory existed, and no one
knew where the cascade would end. From Springfield, Lincoln tried to
manage the crisis. Maybe there was still time for one more compromise.
After all, other slave states, most notably Virginia, still remained in the
Union. Maybe the secessionists would see reason. Some Northerners said
let them go, but that would have meant the end of the experiment in
democratic government that began in 1776 and was given form in 1787.
Through the winter of 1860–61, secessionists held the fate of the nation
in their hands. And on April 12, with the firing on Fort Sumter, they
opted for war.

CHAPTER 2

1861

After South Carolina seceded on December 20, major Robert Anderson, in command of the federal garrison in Charleston Harbor, anticipated an assault by the state militia and moved his troops from Fort Moultrie to Fort Sumter. Anderson was a Kentuckian who supported slavery, but his oath to defend the country took priority. President Buchanan sent a merchant ship, the *Star of the West,* to resupply Anderson and his eighty-two men, but on January 9 secessionists fired on the fort. These shots might have signaled the start of the war, except that the lame-duck president, who opposed secession yet thought the federal government had no right to prevent the states from leaving, had no interest in taking action.

The following week, on January 16, the Senate voted twenty-five to twenty-three, with all Republicans in the majority, to defeat a compromise measure offered by Senator John J. Crittenden of Kentucky. Crittenden proposed a series of constitutional amendments that would extend the Missouri Compromise line to the Pacific, recognize and protect slavery both where it existed and in territories "now held or hereafter acquired," and forbid Congress to interfere with the interstate slave trade, to abolish slavery in Washington, or to pass any future amendments authorizing itself to interfere with slavery.

Shortly thereafter, representatives from the seven states that had seceded made plans to meet in Montgomery, Alabama. They gathered on February 4 and soon adopted a provisional constitution that would be ratified on March 11. Based on the U.S. Constitution, it provided for one six-year term for president. It recognized the "sovereign and independent character" of each state and asserted that no "law denying or impairing the right of property in negro slaves shall be passed." It also forbade protective tariffs. The convention nominated Jefferson Davis as provisional president of the Confederacy. Davis, a U.S. senator from Mississippi who had also served as secretary of war under Franklin Pierce, resigned his seat once his state seceded, and on February 18 delivered his inaugural speech as president.

Davis stressed that the Confederacy was based on the principles of the Declaration and Constitution of the United States, and that the system of government had not changed, only the interpretation of some of its parts. "We have entered upon the career of independence," explained Davis, "and it must be inflexibly pursued. Through many years of controversy with our late associates, the Northern States, we have vainly endeavored to secure tranquility, and to obtain respect for the rights to which we were entitled. As a necessity, not a choice, we have resorted to the remedy of separation; and henceforth our energies must he directed to the conduct of our own affairs, and the perpetuity of the Confederacy which we have formed."[1]

If Davis largely avoided the topic of slavery, his vice president, Alexander Stephens, a friend of Lincoln who had been a Unionist, made explicit the connection between secession and slavery. In a speech delivered in Savannah on March 21, he ridiculed the idea of the equality of the races. "Our new government," Stephens averred, "is founded upon exactly the opposite idea; its foundations are laid, its corner-stone rests, upon the great truth that the negro is not equal to the white man; that slavery, subordination to the superior race, is his natural and normal condition. This, our new government, is the first, in the history of the world, based upon this great physical, philosophical, and moral truth."[2]

On February 11, Lincoln left Springfield for his own inauguration. At various stops along the way to Washington, he spoke only obliquely about "the present national difficulties." In Philadelphia, on February 22, he declared "there is no need of bloodshed and war" and announced "there will be no blood shed unless it be forced upon the Government." He was hoping that Southern Unionists would have time to exert their influence; he was hoping that his promise not to interfere with slavery where it existed would be accepted; he was hoping that the secessionists would understand that under no circumstances would he surrender to their attempt to overturn the results of a national election.[3]

March 4, Inauguration Day, began blustery, but by afternoon the weather had turned clear. Lincoln adjusted his glasses, unfolded his speech, and began to read. He again reassured Southerners that he had neither intention nor authority to interfere with slavery where it existed. More significantly, he announced that "the Union of these States is perpetual." The idea of a perpetual union had only been developed in the years since the nullification crisis, and it held little appeal to those who saw the nation as a compact among states. Lincoln addressed this, too, saying that even if the Union existed as a matter of contract it took all parties to agree to violate it: "no State, upon its own mere motion, can lawfully get out of the Union." "The central idea of secession," he declared, "is the essence of anarchy." Having reaffirmed his constitutional responsibility to defend and preserve the Union, he assured the nation that that there would be no violence or bloodshed "unless it be forced upon the national authority."

Lincoln went on to restate what he had said many times before: that the only *substantial* dispute was that "one section of our country believes slavery is *right*, and ought to be extended, while the other believes it is *wrong*, and ought not to be extended." Note the change from his letter to Stephens wherein Lincoln said it ought to be restricted; the new formulation was slightly softer. He built to a conclusion by reminding Southerners that "physically speaking, we cannot separate," and then he shifted pronouns to "you": "Suppose you go to war, you cannot fight always; and when, after much loss on both sides, and no gain on either, you cease fighting, the identical old questions, as to terms of intercourse, are again upon you. . . . In *your* hands, my dissatisfied fellow countrymen, and not in *mine*, is the momentous issue of civil war."

He started with policy and he closed with poetry: "We are not enemies, but friends. We must not be enemies. Though passion may have strained, it must not break the bonds of affection. The mystic chords of memory, stretching from every battle-field, and patriot grave, to every living heart and hearthstone, all over this broad land, will yet swell the chorus of the Union, when again touched, as surely they will be, by the better angels of our nature."[4]

After Lincoln spoke, Chief Justice Roger Taney administered the oath of office. The president hoped his speech might have done some good, but by the next day he knew that newspapers had responded along sectional lines. Northern papers saw it as conciliatory; Southern papers viewed it as a declaration of war.

Lincoln had little time to wait to see what impact his inaugural address might have. One of the first messages handed to him was news that Major Anderson's provisions at Fort Sumter would soon be exhausted. While Lincoln and his cabinet debated how to proceed, the Confederate government sent peace commissioners to negotiate with secretary of state William Seward. But as each day passed, Fort Sumter became an increasingly important symbol, and on April 10, Brigadier General Pierre Beauregard, under orders from the Confederate cabinet, demanded the fort's surrender before it could be resupplied with food.

On April 12 at 4:30 in the morning, the first mortar shell exploded. On April 13, at 2:30 in the afternoon, Anderson surrendered the garrison. No one was killed during the bombardment. Confederate secretary of state Robert Toombs had warned against this action, predicting "it will lose us every friend at the north. You will wantonly strike a hornet's nest.... It puts us in the wrong. It is fatal." Northerners rallied to the cause and quickly answered Lincoln's call for seventy-five thousand troops.[5]

Lincoln's appeal for state militia troops to deal with the insurrection prompted four additional states to secede: Virginia (April 17), Arkansas (May 6), North Carolina (May 20), and Tennessee (June 8). Before Virginia had decided, Robert E. Lee, a distinguished military veteran and son of a Revolutionary War hero, was offered command of Union forces but declined. On April 20, he resigned from the United States army and instead accepted command of Virginia's militia forces. Lee said, "I cannot raise my hand against my birthplace, my home, my children."[6]

By summer, the Confederacy consisted of eleven states, with a total population of nine million, three and a half million of whom were slaves. Four other slave states, border states on the east and west—Maryland, Delaware, Kentucky, and Missouri—remained in the Union, though thousands of men from these states fought for the Confederacy. In many cases, brothers took opposite sides: one of Senator Crittenden's sons rose to be a general in the Union army; the other became a general in the Confederate army.

The Union consisted of twenty-two states with a population of about twenty-two million people, a half million of whom were slaves. In every way, the North had greater manpower and resources than the South. By war's end, more than two million men of military age would fight for the North as compared to less than a million for the South. Whereas half the men of military age served for the Union, some three-fourths of all Southern white men served in the Confederate military. The Union had vast superiority in resources such as textile mills and iron works and had a well-developed transportation network, especially railroads. The Union could manufacture almost anything it needed. It also outpaced the Confederacy in food production and had an advantage in numbers of horses and mules.[7]

But wars are not fought on paper, and the Confederacy had distinct advantages of its own. To win, the Union armies would have to invade and conquer; Southerners were defending their homes on familiar territory. The Confederacy was huge (750,000 square miles), with a natural terrain of lengthy rivers and mountainous regions that would make it difficult for any army. The Confederate capital, moved from Montgomery to Richmond in May 1861, may have seemed tantalizingly close, but so was Washington to the Confederate army. In the beginning, the Confederacy also had the tacit support of many leaders of European nations, particularly in Great Britain, which was dependent on Southern cotton. Southerners had a stronger military tradition than Northerners, with seven military academies and a firm belief that one rebel could whip ten Yankees. If the Confederacy needed any reassurance that an inferior force fighting a defensive war on familiar terrain could win, they need only look back to the American revolution. "The Southerners," commented one observer, "can never be conquered; they may be killed, but conquered *never.*"[8]

To isolate the Confederacy and prevent it from resupplying, one of Lincoln's first orders was to impose a naval blockade of all Southern ports. It remained in effect throughout the war and became increasingly effective over time, though it raised a delicate issue of international law. Lincoln never recognized the Confederacy. The states that seceded were involved in a domestic insurrection, and the war was an effort to put down a rebellion. As a result, foreign governments would not be legally justified in recognizing the Confederacy and giving it aid. But a blockade is a tactic used by one sovereign nation against another. By imposing it, Lincoln risked inviting other nations into the conflict, a risk he felt was worth taking in order to begin the process of restoring the nation.

The blockade was a key component in the initial military plan proposed by General-in-Chief Winfield Scott, whose long career dated back to the War of 1812 and who had become a hero during the Mexican War. Scott proposed to cordon off the South and then send a flotilla down the

Mississippi to divide and defeat the Confederacy. It was a sound idea, one Jefferson Davis anticipated when he wrote that "to prevent the enemy getting control of the Mississippi and dismembering the Confederacy, we must mainly rely upon maintaining the points already occupied by defensive works; to wit Vicksburg and Port Hudson." Scott wrote that he hoped "to envelop the insurgent States, and bring them to terms with less bloodshed than by any other plan."[9]

The problem with the plan was that it would take time, and most Northerners were impatient for a quick resolution to the conflict. Opponents derisively labeled Scott's strategy the "Anaconda plan," since like the snake it would surround the foe and suffocate it into surrendering. Lincoln also hoped that as the Confederacy became cut off, Southern Unionists, whom he fervently believed constituted a majority of all the Southern states except South Carolina, would rise up and depose the secessionists. In this, he was disappointed.

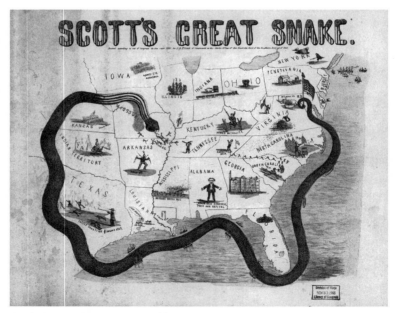

Scott's Great Snake (Cincinnati, 1861). Courtesy of Library of Congress.

On July 4, Lincoln met with Congress in special session and outlined his thinking about a war that had already seen skirmishes in Virginia, Missouri, and elsewhere. Lincoln began by offering a history of what had happened at Fort Sumter and deriding the Confederate argument that the assault was "a matter of self defense on the part of the assailants." The seceding states and they alone, Lincoln thundered, "have forced upon the country, the distinct issue: 'Immediate dissolution, or blood.'" He expressed his hope to make the contest "a short, and a decisive one," and asked Congress for money and men. He reminded his audience that there was no such thing as a right to secession, that such an idea was "an ingenious sophism," and that all Americans who lived by the rule of law must understand that what the nation faced was a domestic insurrection. He expressed his regret at having to employ the war powers of his office, but his only choice was to "perform this duty, or surrender the existence of the government." The latter, he pledged, he would never do.[10]

"It makes my heart sick," wrote a young man from Tennessee, "to think of the State of our once happy and yet beloved country for there is no history that tells of any country that was ever happyer than ours—and now to see two brave and warlike armies armed with all the deadly instruments that art and wealth could procure marching over our once peaceable country and to think when they meet in the bloody battlefields what destruction...and what misery they can produce."[11]

As the July heat mounted, believing that a decisive Union victory might accelerate the end of the rebellion, Lincoln ordered an assault against the Confederate army near Manassas, Virginia. Beauregard, who had been given command of Confederate forces after his success at Fort Sumter, had an army of twenty thousand men that threatened Washington, some twenty-five miles away. Union General Irvin McDowell had thirty-five thousand men under his command, and although he was nervous about proceeding with men so lacking in experience, the advance began on July 16. The march proved chaotic, made worse, no doubt, by the unavailability of any reliable maps of Virginia. With the help of good intelligence and by moving units around, the Confederate army was able to prepare itself for the assault.[12]

On Sunday, July 21, McDowell reached his destination and prepared to attack. Curious spectators from Washington, thinking it would make a pleasant day's entertainment to watch the Union forces fight, arrived in carriages. The initial assault looked promising, but it was repelled when Confederate reinforcements arrived. Late in the afternoon, the rebels launched a counterattack. Their determined rush forward and piercing yell, like the howl of "a thousand dogs," forced a frantic, disorganized retreat by Union military and civilians alike. It didn't help that uniforms this early in the war had not been standardized and Northern troops mistook Confederates in blue for Union men. In the end, on both sides, hundreds were killed and well over a thousand were wounded. Far worse was yet to come.[13]

Reading reports of the battle in London, Henry Adams, serving as secretary to his father, Charles Francis Adams, minister to England, wrote that "Bull's Run will be a by-word of ridicule for all time...the disgrace is frightful....If this happens again, farewell to our country for many a day." Lincoln reacted by demoting McDowell and bringing in George McClellan to command the forces now named the Army of the Potomac. McClellan was young and ambitious. He was also a Democrat who came to believe "I have become *the* power of the land" and privately labeled Lincoln "the original gorilla." Whatever his megalomaniacal tendencies, he knew how to train and organize an army that grew to over one hundred thousand men, and he spent much of the rest of the year in preparation. In November, Winfield Scott retired, and Lincoln promoted McClellan to commander of all Union forces.[14]

Lincoln soon faced a delicate political and military issue when, on August 30, General John C. Fremont, commander of the western department of the Union effort, issued a proclamation that placed Missouri under martial law and declared free the slaves in that state who belonged to supporters of the rebellion. Fremont, who had been the first Republican nominee for president in 1856, was called a hero by those aching to see the war quickly transformed into a war against slavery. One writer anointed him "the people's first leader against the great slaveholders' conspiracy."[15]

Lincoln was upset. He told the general that the clause freeing the slaves was "objectionable." It violated the terms of the Crittenden-Johnson resolution, passed by Congress on July 25, which reaffirmed the position that the war was not being fought to overthrow or interfere with established institutions. It also did not conform to the terms of a Confiscation Act, signed on August 6, which provided for the confiscation of slaves only if they were being used directly in support of the insurrection. Reaction to Fremont's proclamation threatened the delicate balance with those border states still in the Union. Indeed, if it stood, Kentucky seemed very likely to secede from the Union. The proclamation itself violated Lincoln's assurance that he had no intentions of interfering with slavery where it existed. After Fremont refused to modify the order, Lincoln revoked it and eventually removed Fremont from command.[16]

But the issue of the slaves as a matter of military policy was not driven only by the wishes of commanders. As early as May, General Benjamin Butler reported that several slaves had escaped Confederate lines and arrived at Fort Monroe, Virginia. He dubbed them "contraband of war," and for the rest of the war runaway slaves who presented themselves to Union lines were known as contrabands. By July, there were nearly a thousand of them in Butler's camp. These contrabands seemed to fit uneasily, however, under the terms of the Confiscation Act. Northern Democrats were displeased, as were conservative Republicans, but abolitionists hoped events would transform Union war aims into a struggle against slavery. Charles Loring Brace, a leading reformer and founder of the Children's Aid Society, wrote that when "a National Declaration of Emancipation to the slave...has been widely scattered and proclaimed, and the slaves understand it—as they would marvelously soon—we have a nation of allies in the enemy's ranks. There is a foe in every Southerner's household." Frederick Douglass, an electrifying orator and writer whose published account of his travails as a slave had opened Northern eyes in 1845, proclaimed in May that the "'inexorable logic of events'" would force upon the administration and American people an awareness that "the war now being waged in this land is a war for and against slavery." In time, runaway slaves would help make it so.[17]

From the start of the war, slavery also played a critical role in diplomatic relations. The Confederacy was eager to win European recognition and support. Most European governments were antislavery and this played a role in keeping them from rushing to the Confederacy's aid, though they certainly desired the cotton imports. Furthermore, foreign governments didn't want to side with a losing cause, so they waited to see how the military conflict would proceed. Diplomacy on both sides was vigorous, especially in regard to Great Britain, which was deeply affected by the American conflict and whose aristocracy tended to be sympathetic toward the South, whereas its working classes supported the North. When on May 14 the British government recognized the belligerent status of the Confederacy, which allowed the South to borrow money and purchase nonmilitary supplies, the Union feared this was a first step toward official diplomatic recognition.

An event toward the end of the year nearly brought Great Britain into the war on the Confederate side. On November 8, Captain Charles Wilkes of the

United States warship *San Jacinto* boarded a British vessel, the *Trent,* and removed two Confederate commissioners, James Mason of Virginia and John Slidell of Louisiana, headed to Europe on a diplomatic mission. The Confederate commissioners, who had instructions to argue that the blockade was illegal whereas secession was legal, and that Great Britain would benefit from a Confederate victory, were brought to a prison in Boston.

The British government reacted with indignation. Lord Palmerston, the prime minister, considered it "a deliberate and premeditated insult" intended to provoke England. One writer informed Seward, "the people are frantic with rage, and were the country polled I fear 999 men out of one thousand would declare for immediate war." Lincoln's administration responded by saying that Wilkes had acted without authorization. The two prisoners were released on New Year's Day and made their way to Europe. For the time being, the war remained an internal affair between the United States and the Confederate States.[18]

Addressing the Confederate Congress on November 18, Jefferson Davis spoke positively about the course of the war for the Confederacy: "A succession of glorious victories at Bethel, Bull Run, Manassas, Springfield, Lexington, Leesburg, and Belmont, has checked the wicked invasion which greed of gain and the unhallowed lust of power brought upon our soil, and has proved that numbers cease to avail when directed against a people fighting for the sacred right of self-government and the privileges of freemen." Of course, Davis conveniently neglected some important Union victories in western Virginia and along the South's Atlantic coast, but this speech was meant to be inspirational. He concluded with a discussion of the *Trent* affair, restating his belief that the blockade was a farce and requesting "a recognized place in the great family of nations."[19]

Lincoln sent his annual message to Congress on December 3. He addressed the question of foreign involvement and observed that "a nation which endures factious domestic division, is exposed to disrespect abroad; and one party, if not both, is sure, sooner or later, to invoke foreign intervention." As for the commercial reasons that might induce European involvement, Lincoln reminded Congress that it was the intact Union that made for valuable commerce, and not "the same nation broken into hostile fragments." He reaffirmed his decision not to hastily employ "radical and extreme measures" that would affect loyal citizens as well as disloyal ones, and expressed his anxiety that the conflict with the seceded states "not degenerate into a violent and remorseless revolutionary struggle." In 1862, he would change his mind about the first and see the second come to pass.[20]

CHAPTER 3

1862

In early January, Lincoln met with Montgomery Meigs, the quartermaster general of the Union army. The depressed president told Meigs, "The people are impatient; Chase has no money, and he tells me he can raise no money; the Gen. of the army has typhoid fever. The bottom is out of the tub. What shall I do?" On January 27, he issued General War Order Number 1, which commanded the forward movement of all troops by Washington's Birthday.[1]

In February, uplifting news arrived from the western theater of military operation. Confederate general Albert Sidney Johnston commanded forces stretching four hundred miles across Kentucky, Tennessee, Mississippi, Alabama, and Georgia. Union command of the Department of Missouri was led by Henry Halleck, whose book *Elements of Military Art and Science* Lincoln had been reading. Don Carlos Buell, head of the Department of the Ohio, had orders to move into Tennessee, and while he was slow to act, another general, Ulysses S. Grant, who commanded the district of Southeast Missouri, was not.

After graduating from the United States Military Academy, Grant had served in the Mexican War, but he resigned his commission in 1854 under suspicion of drinking on duty. He farmed and clerked until the outbreak of war gave him another chance at success. He was described as short and round-shouldered; one soldier said of him that "he habitually wears an expression as if he had determined to drive his head through a brick wall." On February 6, in conjunction with a fleet of gunboats, Grant attacked Fort Henry on the Tennessee River, taking it on the same day. Grant then moved on Fort Donelson, twelve miles away on the Cumberland River. After several days of vigorous back-and-forth fighting, on February 16, Donelson fell on the only terms Grant would accept: "unconditional and immediate surrender" of its twelve thousand men. With this act, the initials U. S. Grant gained new meaning. The Union now controlled two main rivers and had a direct line to Nashville, which the Confederates would soon evacuate.[2]

Celebrations erupted as news of the victories spread across the Union. Church bells rang and cannons were fired. One editorial declared that for failing to join in the festivities, "any person found sober after nine o'clock in the evening would be arrested as a secessionist." Writing from London in March, Henry Adams reported "the talk of intervention, only two months ago so loud as to take a semi-official tone, is now out of the mouths of everyone." Southerners were shocked by the "disgraceful" and "shameful" losses, and knew that the defeats harmed their case abroad. On February 22, Jefferson Davis delivered an inauguration address and acknowledged that "we too have had our trials and our difficulties." But although "the tide for the moment is against us, the final result in our favor is not doubtful."[3]

Whatever joy Lincoln might have felt was quickly dashed by the tragic death of his eleven-year-old son, Willie, from typhoid fever. The minister who delivered the funeral sermon spoke of "the dark shadow of affliction" that had fallen on the Lincolns. It had fallen as well on the nation. Two years later, Jefferson Davis would also lose a son, who fell from the second floor of the Confederate executive mansion. Both these leaders suffered acutely from the rising tide of death and both knew personally what parents had to endure.

The worst death toll in a single battle to that point came on April 6, near Shiloh Church, Tennessee. Johnston, united now with Beauregard, surprised Union forces under the command of William T. Sherman. In a brutal day of fighting, Union forces were driven back, but Grant, reinforced by General Don Carlos Buell's Army of the Ohio, arrived late in the day. Johnston was mortally wounded. A counterattack the next day won back the ground lost, and Beauregard, now in command, retreated. Men on both sides were exhausted, having marched and fought for days through mud and rain without nourishment.

The battle marked the emergence of Sherman as a valuable asset to Grant. To that point, Sherman's career had been checkered. After West Point, the Ohioan had served in California during the Mexican War. He then wandered on to various occupations: banker, lawyer, railroad man, superintendent of a military college. His military service in Kentucky as commander of the Department of the Cumberland in the fall of 1861 went off kilter and, perhaps overcome by stress, he took a leave. He returned to Grant's Army of the Tennessee as a division commander, and by force of will became a warrior.

Shiloh put an end to any Northern hopes of a quick resolution to the war. One soldier, who earlier predicted the rebellion would end in six months, now wrote in his diary, "if my life is spared I will continue in my country's service until this rebellion is put down, should it be ten years." Grant was roundly criticized, and rumors spread that he had been drinking. But Lincoln stood by the general.[4]

More than three thousand died in the battle, and over sixteen thousand were wounded. One reason for the lethal results of Civil War battles was the shift away from smoothbore muskets to rifled barrels that fired new bullets, called Minie balls, that had greater accuracy and range. One soldier observed, "those Minie, Sharp, & Enfield balls tear a terrible hole. Their weight & velocity is so great that bones stand a poor chance. Out of any given number of men who are shot in battle it is said that twice as many dies who are struck by these balls as among those who are hit by the ordinary musket balls." Grant would later write that the battlefield "was so covered with dead that it would have been possible to walk across the clearing, in any direction, stepping on dead bodies, without a foot touching the ground." A Confederate soldier said, "it was too shocking too horrible." Herman Melville later wrote a poem about Shiloh that contained these lines:[5]

> Foemen at morn, but friend at eve—
> Fame or country least their care:
> (What like a bullet can undeceive!)

Across North and South, the war quickly dashed any romantic ideals that had led Americans to believe glory and honor were to be found on the battlefield. After Shiloh, one Union artilleryman from Illinois wrote to his father: "will spare you the horrid and disgusting details of the thousands of suffering wounded, and mangled corpses I saw....We have at last had our wish for a hard battle gratified and never again do I expect to hear the same wish from the lips of our men. We are just as ready now to do our duty as we were, but to desire another hard battle, with the same chances of loss to our company, is quite a different thing."[6]

The war would be neither brief nor limited. After Shiloh, terror grew. A year into the conflict, Americans were beginning to realize just how bloody a price would be paid, not for glory but for peace.

The artilleryman's letter indirectly raised the issue of what soldiers thought they were fighting for during the war. "To do our duty," is vague, though once in the military, fighting for one's unit, one another, and out of fear of being seen as cowardly certainly kept many a man going forward. Seeing one's friends slaughtered added another potent motivator: "My heart was rilled with hatred and revenge against the enemy....I could not restrain my tears and felt that I would hazard my life in any position to mow down their ranks with canister. After this I had a feeling of utmost indifference as to my fate."[7]

Other generalizations about the motivations of each side can be suggested. *Rage militaire* drove men to arms when appeals to patriotism crested. In the Union, hundreds of thousands of immigrants, as much as a quarter of the military, enlisted. Undoubtedly, they saw service as an opportunity to support the country they hoped to make their own. Many Irish, Scots, and German immigrants joined together and formed their own regiments. Whether immigrants or natives, men signed up to support the government in its contest against "anarchy and revolution."

Few mentioned hostility to slavery as the reason for enlisting, though some spoke of opposition to the slave power. And they spoke generally about liberty and the need to preserve the Union. Over time, however, some began to write about the need to eliminate slavery to achieve these goals. In January 1862, one soldier, a private in the Fifth Iowa, declared, "I believe that Slavery (the worst of all curses) is the sole cause of this Rebellion and until this cause is removed and slavery abolished the rebellion will continue to exist."[8]

Confederate soldiers also cited the abstractions of liberty and self-determination, but added to the mixture questions of honor in the defense of their homeland against invasion by an enemy bent on subjugating them. Time and again they said they were fighting for their "rights," which also meant the right for some of them to own slaves. One soldier wrote that he would "rather die the Death of a brave and truehearted Southern soldier than to see my country trodden down by the Northern invader." All the men, he proclaimed, "will spill the last drop of blood in their veins before they will submit to the Federal Government."[9]

And yet the two sides often fraternized while on picket duty, exchanging newspapers and goods (coffee for tobacco was a favorite) and sometimes whistling alternate notes of tunes to one another. After trading "canteens and carterages [*sic*]" one Union soldier wrote "now you might think it strange but I cant help but be just friendly to one of them as I would to one of my own country." On December 23, Charles Haydon, a Union lieutenant colonel, recorded the following in his diary:

> This m'g one of their pickets called to one of ours, "I say Yank what are you fighting about?" "I don't know." "Say Reb what are you fighting about?" "I don't know." "Let's throw our guns into the river & end the d——d war."[10]

Both sides suffered from the ordeals of soldiering: long, exhausting marches in shoes that blistered the feet ("found one of our men dead at noon laying by the fence. He had been marched so hard that he fell over dead"); rations that were often barely edible ("two cups of muddy coffee & a few squares of hard tack per day"); lice-infested clothes and bouts of illness, especially fevers and diarrhea (one soldier concocted a potion consisting of "blackberry roots and sweet bark gum boiled down to a syrup and sweetened" to ease diarrhea). And camp was filled with temptation and vice, whether drinking, gambling, cursing, or the visits of prostitutes. One exasperated officer exclaimed, "if the men pursue the enemy as vigorously as they do whores they will make very efficient soldiers."

Fear was a constant, dealt with in different ways, whether the bravado of willing to die for one's country or the fatalism that God's will would be done or the actions of soldiers who seemed to disappear once the firing began. What they saw and did changed them. Men "curse, swear, and play cards all night in a tent where there is a corpse," wrote a Confederate officer. Another acknowledged that he experienced a change such that "I look on the carcass of a man now with pretty much such feeling as I would do were it a horse or hog." A Union soldier observed after one battle that the "sun rose bright and clear this morning to spread his brilliant light over thousands of mangled human bodies."[11]

Soldiers wrote frequently about the aftermath of battles: "The dead lay in all postures...one I saw on his hands & knees with his head shot off. Two men were found lying opposite each other with each his bayonet through the other's body....A few of the dead remain unburied. They are so bloated as to burst open the legs of their pants & the sleeves of their coats. Their features are entirely obliterated & the face when not consumed by maggots is but a smooth, dark shining mass of putridity." In 1865, one sergeant confessed, "I cannot write anymore long letters like I used to. I do not feel like the same person I was a year ago." A captain reflected, "I do actually believe that I have forgotten how to act look or walk like a civilian."[12]

The terrors of war notwithstanding, armies needed men, and in April the Confederate Congress passed a law making males between the ages of eighteen and thirty-five subject to conscription. A supplemental act later in the year exempted one white man for every twenty slaves on a plantation and provided for the purchasing of substitutes, which favored the wealthy and led some to call the conflict "a rich man's war but a poor man's fight." Facing the draft, even after initially volunteering and serving, many men "chose" to reenlist. As one Confederate soldier put it in a letter home, "Pa, we have all reenlisted for the 'War.' We had to do it and I thought I would come on as a patriot soldier of the South."[13]

The Conscription Act exposed a deep ideological flaw in the Confederacy. States had seceded to control their own destiny and to remove themselves from centralized authority. But it took a nationalized command to run a war, and the demands of the government often conflicted with the desires of states. Georgia's governor, Joseph E. Brown, for example, objected vigorously to the law and called conscription "subversive of [Georgia's] sovereignty, and at war with all the principles for the support of which Georgia entered into this revolution." The longer the war threatened to last, the more resistance the individual states might demonstrate. It had been a long time since the Confederate victory at Manassas; losses in Missouri, Kentucky, western Virginia, Tennessee, and even New Mexico left Southerners fearing the worst.[14]

The longer the war went on, the more the U.S. Congress legislated what could not have passed while Southern Democrats were in the Union, and in the process remade the nation according to the Republican ideal of a liberal, capitalist society populated by educated, independent landowners. The Homestead Act (signed May 20) provided land to applicants willing to develop the acreage in return for which, after five years, they would gain title; the Morrill Land Grant Act (signed July 2) gave states thousands of acres of land for the development of agricultural and mechanical schools; the National Banking Act (signed February 25, 1863; revised in 1864) created a national currency and charters for a system of national banks and served to help finance the war.

Congressional debate on these issues came in the midst of a spring campaign against Richmond. Lincoln was anxious for McClellan to move forward. On February 27, he lamented that the "general does not intend to do anything." On April 9, he wrote to McClellan: "it is indispensable to *you* that you strike a blow. *I* am powerless to help this...*you must act.*" McClellan's Peninsula Campaign had actually begun in March. The battle at Hampton Roads on March 8–9 between two ironclad ships, the Union *Monitor* against the Confederate *Virginia*, ended inconclusively but forever transformed naval warfare. In late March, an armada of tens of thousands of men sailed from Alexandria to Fortress Monroe. McClellan had superior forces to the Confederate army (the Army of the Potomac had 105,000 men; Richmond was defended by 60,000), but he balked from attacking under the mistaken belief that the Southern army was at least equally strong.[15]

Although Union forces gained access to the James River, McClellan made only halting progress toward Richmond, or in subduing Confederate forces under the command of Joseph E. Johnston, who was wounded on May 31 at the Battle of Seven Pines. Two days of fighting yielded heavy casualties (a total of more than eleven thousand) but little change in position. The most important result for the future of the war was that the wounded Johnston was replaced by Robert E. Lee, who renamed his command the Army of Northern Virginia.

Lee would soon develop a mystique that intimidated Union men and made him revered by rebels. Formal, poised, gentlemanly, after the war he would be venerated. A Union sergeant wrote, "I think old Lee is too sharp for our men"—a typical expression of the beliefs of Union soldiers. Even toward war's end, Southerners would not criticize the General. "What a position does he occupy," exulted one woman, "the idol, the point of trust, of confidence & repose of thousands." Lee's reputation undoubtedly shaped the military conflict, but it cut both ways. While his audacity and standing, along with the belief in the martial superiority of the rebels, may have cost the Union in battle, over time it is likely that Lee's willingness to take questionable offensive chances stemmed in part from a belief in his army's invincibility.[16]

The Peninsula Campaign concluded with a series of savage engagements known collectively as the Seven Days Battles, fought between June 25 and July 1. The sixth and final battle took place at Malvern Hill, where Lee attacked an entrenched Union position and paid for it with heavy casualties. "It was not war—it was murder," agonized one Confederate general. Despite victory, McClellan pulled back, and Richmond was no longer threatened.[17]

Through the spring, with Johnston and Lee fighting on the peninsula, Thomas Jackson, nicknamed "Stonewall" after his heroics at Bull Run, led a campaign through the Shenandoah Valley. A graduate of the United States Military Academy and a former professor at the Virginia Military Institute, Jackson distinguished himself as one of the most imaginative and daring Confederate generals. A series of victories at such places as Front Royal, Winchester, Cross Keys, and Port Republic left Jackson in control of the valley and in a position to reinforce Lee's armies at Richmond. He moved vigorously across the valley, defeated a larger but divided enemy army, and gave an enormous boost to Confederate confidence in the aftermath of defeats in the west.

And yet the Confederates felt they should have accomplished more. On July 9, Lee wrote to his wife: "Our success has not been as great or complete as we could have desired, but God knows what is best for us."[18] McClellan's army was there for the breaking. But at other points, so, too, was Lee's. In the aftermath, both sides scrutinized what they might have done differently. But there is so much in war that no one can control: the weather, communication, intelligence, organization, and just plain luck. Only Jackson's campaign seemed pristine, a model of a general in perfect command, executed with bravado.

Lincoln longed to find what was best for the Union cause. Unable to sleep, losing weight, he tried to maintain a positive attitude, but the only unadulterated good news all spring had been the capture of New Orleans by Admiral David Farragut in late April. On July 7, Lincoln traveled to Harrison's Landing, a stretch of five miles or so on the east side of the James River, to see McClellan and visit the troops.

McClellan presented Lincoln with a letter explaining that he thought the war "should be conducted upon the highest principles known to Christian Civilization. It should not be a War looking to the subjugation of the people of any state, in any event. It should not be, at all, a War upon population; but against armed forces and political organizations.

Neither confiscation of property, political executions of persons, territorial organization of states or forcible abolition of slavery should be contemplated for a moment."[19]

Lincoln already knew McClellan's attitudes toward the war. The general consistently overestimated the enemy's troop strength and was reluctant to commit his men to battle. He had become a master of inactivity. And he seemed unwilling to take any actions that might be seen as unchivalrous by Southerners. In June, for example, McClellan would not allow wounded soldiers to use an estate owned by Mrs. Robert E. Lee as a military hospital. McClellan said he had made a promise, and Lincoln apparently told a noted physician, "I will break it for him."[20]

On July 11, Lincoln named Halleck general-in-chief of all land forces. The change in command marked the beginning of a change in strategy. The war would be prosecuted more energetically and aggressively. The property of civilians would become a legitimate military target, and the struggle began its shift from a war against an enemy army to a war against a people in rebellion.

Lincoln and Congress also began gradually but systematically to attack slavery. On March 6, Lincoln asked Congress to adopt a joint resolution stating that the government would cooperate with any state that adopted an act of gradual emancipation. He had in mind the slave states still in the Union and hoped that by taking steps to eliminate slavery these states would shatter Confederate hopes that they would eventually join in the rebel cause. Lincoln was careful to say that his proposal "sets up no claim of a right, by federal authority, to interfere with slavery within state limits." He merely hoped to accelerate the process by offering pecuniary aid. Congress passed the resolution, but the border states did not accept the offer.[21]

A week later, Congress took a decisive step by passing an article of war that prohibited officers from returning escaped slaves to their masters, even if they were loyal to the Union. Any officer found guilty of violating the act would be court-martialed. This had the effect of expanding the terms of the Confiscation Act of August 1861.

Congress was not done. On April 16, Lincoln signed an act abolishing slavery in Washington, D.C. More than three thousand slaves received their freedom, but, much to the dismay of radical Republicans, the government compensated the owners for their loss and set aside money to promote colonization. Still, the blemish of slavery on the capital of the republic had been removed. "At the national capital Slavery will give way to Freedom," exulted Charles Sumner, "but the good work will not stop here. It must proceed. What God and Nature decree, Rebellion cannot arrest."[22]

A month later, some of Lincoln's most ardent antislavery supporters were dismayed when the president rescinded General David Hunter's General Order Number 11, which had declared the slaves in South Carolina, Georgia, and Florida "forever free." Hunter's action enraged Southerners and Northern Democrats and led Jefferson Davis to offer a bounty for his capture and execution. Lincoln's action, however, had nothing to do with his attitudes toward the abolition of slavery; instead, he rescinded the order out of his belief that only the executive, not any of his officers, could make such policy. Several months later, he would put the matter this way: "as commander-in-chief of the army and navy, in time of war, I suppose I have a right to take any measure which may best subdue the enemy."[23]

Lincoln took the opportunity in his May 19 message about Hunter to remind the border states of his earlier message to Congress encouraging them to adopt a plan of gradual emancipation and imploring them not to be "blind to the signs of the times." Congress had been taking action; the president had been taking action; the generals had been taking action (without authority but still acting); and the slaves themselves had been taking action by making their way to Union lines.

Yet still, to many, it seemed that not nearly enough was being done. On July 5, one woman wrote to a family member that "as things stand the South is fighting to maintain slavery, and the North is trying to fight so as not to put it down." On July 12, Lincoln appealed again to border-state members of Congress to adopt a plan for gradual, compensated emancipation. He tried reasoning with them: now they had a chance to get something in return for their property, whereas if the struggle continued slavery would be gone "by the mere incidents of the war." He noted that in regard to the issue of emancipation, "the pressure, in this direction, is still upon me, and is increasing."[24]

Twenty of the twenty-seven congressmen from the border states rejected his plea, however, and on the next day, July 13, riding in a carriage on the way to a funeral for the infant son of Edwin Stanton, his secretary of war, Lincoln confided to Seward and Gideon Welles, the secretary of the navy, that he had decided to act against slavery. He told his cabinet members that "he had about come to the conclusion that we must free the slaves or be ourselves subdued."[25]

Lincoln informed his entire cabinet of the decision and read a draft of the proclamation to them on July 22. His action was inspired partly by the passage of the Second Confiscation Act. It included a provision that proclaimed that all slaves of owners engaged in rebellion "shall be forever free of their servitude, and not again held as slaves." Lincoln still doubted congressional authority over slavery in the states. And seeing it as a bill of attainder, he even considered vetoing the Act. Instead, he planned to ground emancipation as an executive decision. On the advice of Seward, he decided to await a Union military victory so as to bolster Northern morale, minimize the opposition that inevitably would come from Northern Democrats, and not make it seem as if emancipation was a desperate act on the part of a teetering government.

Somehow, word of Lincoln's decision did not leak. Given the events of the year, radical Republicans railed against Lincoln's inaction on slavery. On August 20, Horace Greeley, the influential editor of the *New York Tribune*, published an open letter to Lincoln titled "The Prayer of Twenty Millions." He informed the president that Northerners were "sorely disappointed and deeply pained by the policy you seem to be pursuing with regard to the slaves of the Rebels" and implored him to stop his "deference to Rebel slavery," enforce the Confiscation Act, and take executive action against the institution.[26]

Lincoln responded on August 22: "My paramount object in this struggle *is* to save the Union, and it is *not* either to save or to destroy slavery. If I could save the union without freeing *any* slave I would do it, and if I could do it by freeing *all* the slaves I would do it; and if I could save it by freeing some and leaving others alone I would also do that." It was a crafty response, designed not to alienate Southern sympathizers and aimed at reaffirming what he had been saying from the start about the preservation of the Union. It was easy for men like Greeley not to notice the change suggested by the line "if I could do it by freeing *all* the slaves I would do it." Lincoln hadn't said that before.[27]

Radical Republicans did not appreciate what they saw as waffling on the part of the president. Frederick Douglass denounced Lincoln for "making himself appear silly and ridiculous...he has been unusually garrulous, characteristically foggy, remarkably illogical and untimely in his utterances."[28]

Despite Lincoln's hopes, a Union military victory was not quick in coming. Instead, the Confederates gained a significant triumph when Lee attacked again at Bull Run. This second battle began with Stonewall

Jackson cutting off the Union supply line at Manassas. In a battle that raged from August 28 to August 30, Union general John Pope was outsmarted and outmaneuvered by Lee, Jackson, and James Longstreet, whose forces arrived in time to reinforce the Confederate line. Longstreet's force of twenty-eight thousand counterattacked and drove the Union forces back for over a mile. Sixteen thousand of Pope's sixty thousand men were killed, wounded, or missing; the Confederates suffered some nine thousand casualties out of fifty thousand men. It was a humiliating, demoralizing defeat for the Union. "For the first time I believe it possible that Washington may be taken," wrote the correspondent for the *New York Tribune.* An officer confessed: "our men are sick of war. They fight without an aim and without enthusiasm." Lincoln fell into depression. One cabinet member described him as "wrung by the bitterest anguish—said he felt almost ready to hang himself."[29]

Southerners were elated and saw it as a time to press the advantage. Lee wrote to Davis on September 3 that "the present seems to be the most propitious time, since the commencement of the war, for the Confederate army to enter Maryland." That invasion would culminate on September 17 in the Battle of Antietam. McClellan's Army of the Potomac battled Lee's Army of Northern Virginia through a day that saw repeated attacks and counterattacks and missed opportunities to exploit advantages. The combat ended with combined casualties of over twenty-three thousand. Each side suffered more than two thousand battlefield dead, and thousands more would perish from their wounds. It remains the single bloodiest day in American military history. Afterward, a New Hampshire surgeon wrote to his wife, "when I think of the battle of Antietam it seems so strange. Who permits it? To see or feel that a power is in existence that can and will hurl masses of men against each other in deadly conflict— slaying each other by the thousands—mangling and deforming their fellow men is almost impossible. But it is so and why we cannot know."[30]

The battle was a strategic victory for the Union, as Lee was forced to return to Virginia. Five days later, Lincoln used the occasion to issue a preliminary Emancipation Proclamation. The document declared that as of January 1, all slaves held in states then in rebellion would be "forever free." It cited the article of war adopted by Congress on March 13 and the Second Confiscation Act passed on July 17. The document also reiterated the president's goal of helping states to adopt plans of abolition and supporting the "effort to colonize persons of African descent."

Lincoln still clung to colonization as a panacea for the race problem in America. On August 14, he had met with a "Committee of Colored Men" and told them that "even when you cease to be slaves, you are yet far removed from being placed on an equality with the white race." He deplored the ill effects of slavery on white men and argued that "without the institution of Slavery and the colored race as a basis, the war could not have an existence." "It is better for us both," he urged, "to be separated," and he offered to invest government money in helping to establish a new colony in Central America. Nothing substantial came of the proposal. Privately, Salmon Chase, secretary of the treasury, snorted, "how much better would be a manly protest against prejudice against color!"[31]

As might be expected, reactions to the preliminary Emancipation Proclamation ran the gamut. Governors of most of the Union states congratulated the president. Even those politicians who sought a more immediate and direct assault on the institution expressed enthusiasm. Sumner said, "it is enough for me that in the exercise of the war power, it strikes at the origin and mainspring of the Rebellion." Horace Greeley instantly buried whatever ill feelings he had toward Lincoln and said, "it is the beginning of the end of the rebellion; the beginning of the new life of the nation." A Union captain noted that "though the President carefully calls it nothing but a war measure, yet it is the beginning of a great reform and the first blow struck at the real, original cause of the war." Disappointed, however, that there had been no spike in enlistments, on September 28, Lincoln wrote to his vice president, Hannibal Hamlin, that "the North responds to the proclamation sufficiently in breath; but breath alone kills no rebels."[32]

Whereas Northern Republicans by and large praised the act (although some questioned its constitutionality), most Northern Democrats, such as New York's governor, Horatio Seymour, described it as a "bloody, barbarous, revolutionary, and unconstitutional scheme." They were also dismayed by a second proclamation issued two days later that suspended the writ of habeas corpus, thereby giving the government broad powers to arrest "disloyal" citizens who interfered in the war, particularly with the raising of troops.[33]

Southerners denounced the Emancipation Proclamation as "a call for the insurrection of four million slaves, and the inauguration of a reign of hell upon earth." Jefferson Davis said it afforded "the complete and crowning proof of the true nature of the designs of the party which elevated" Lincoln to office. The *Charleston Mercury* saw the act as a "stroke of desperate statesmanship" issued by a crazed president beholden to radical abolitionists. The paper also realized that it was a barrier to European recognition. The war was now clearly a war against slavery, and European nations would be extra cautious about entering the fray, though the initial reaction of foreign statesmen was tepid because they believed the Proclamation tacitly supported slave insurrection.[34]

The Emancipation Proclamation could not mask the reality that the war had not been going well for the Union. The armies had suffered costly defeats, the treasury was low on money (Congress had imposed the first federal income tax), and enlistments were down. Many Northerners were experiencing "war weariness," and Lincoln's proclamations on emancipation and habeas corpus energized Peace Democrats (derogatorily called Copperheads by Republicans who saw them as poisonous snakes waiting to rear up and bite). Even though Republicans gained five Senate seats, the results of the fall congressional elections were disheartening for Lincoln's party: Democrats had a net gain of twenty-eight seats. They won the governorships of New York and New Jersey and the state houses in New Jersey, Illinois, and Indiana. They even carried Lincoln's home district.

In the midst of the fall elections, thousands in New York had a chance to see the war in a way they hadn't previously—through photographs. The Civil War was the first widely photographed war, and photographers of the North and the South captured tens of thousands of images of soldiers, armaments, and battlefields. Shutter speed was still too slow to record action, but the images that were circulated in galleries and on small photographic cards known as "carte de visites" gave Americans far away from the conflict what seemed like a firsthand view of the nature of war.

Matthew Brady was the main impresario of his day, and his gallery on Broadway in New York City advertised an exhibition called "The Dead of Antietam." Two photographers in his employ, Alexander Gardner and James Gibson, had arrived at Antietam two days after the battle. Their photographs were the first to show dead bodies, some lying alone in the field, others lined up for burial. A reporter for the *New York Times* visited the gallery and on October 20 offered a review:

> The dead of the battle-field come to us very rarely, even in dreams. We see the list in the morning paper at breakfast, but dismiss its recollection with the coffee....Mr. Brady has done something to bring

home to us the terrible reality and earnestness of war. If he has not brought bodies and laid them in our door-yards and along streets, he has done something very like it.... We should scarce choose to be in the gallery, when one of the women bending over them should recognize a husband, a son, or a brother in the still, lifeless lines of bodies, that lie ready for the gaping trenches.... Homes have been made desolate, and the light of life in thousands of hearts has been quenched forever. All of this desolation, imagination must paint[,] for broken hearts cannot be photographed.[35]

The images destroyed any romantic notions about the war—it was all too real, and clearly something needed to be done soon to bring it to an end. Lincoln continued to press McClellan to follow up on the victory at Antietam; finally, on November 7, he relieved McClellan of command of the Army of the Potomac in favor of Ambrose Burnside, a West Point graduate who took the new position reluctantly.

On December 12, the Union army crossed the Rappahannock River and the next day repeatedly assaulted a dug-in Confederate position on Prospect Hill and Marye's Heights near Fredricksburg. Burnside's men time and

Confederate Dead by a Fence on the Hagerstown Road (Antietam, 1862). Courtesy of Library of Congress.

again tried to take the Heights, but Lee's men were shielded by a four-foot-high wall four hundred yards long. By nightfall, the bodies of Union troops littered the terrain. The Union absorbed more than twelve thousand casualties; the Confederates fewer than five thousand. Lee apparently said, "it is well that war is so horrible, or else we should grow too fond of it."[36]

At year's end, Jefferson Davis, who was home in Mississippi for Christmas, gave a speech in which he admitted that "the contest has assumed proportions more gigantic than I had anticipated" and denounced the Yankee war "waged for the gratification of the lust of power and of aggrandizement, for your conquest and subjugation, with a malignant ferocity and with a disregard and a contempt of the usages of civilization, entirely unequalled in history." He was especially appalled by Lincoln's preliminary Emancipation Proclamation, which promised, Davis believed, to ignite servile insurrection across the South. Still, he felt the war was the Confederates' to be won. Given that "we have entered upon a conflict with a nation contiguous to us in territory, and vastly superior to us in numbers,...the wonder is not that we have done little, but that we have done so much."[37]

As the year came to a close, some wondered, given the fall election results and the Union's military reverses, whether Lincoln would stand by his promise to issue on January 1 the Emancipation Proclamation, a proclamation made necessary in part by what the Confederacy had accomplished. On December 1, he elaborated at length on schemes of emancipation in his annual message to Congress and made clear that the time had come to act, to break with what had come before, because "the dogmas of the quiet past, are inadequate to the stormy present," and that by "*giving* freedom to the *slave*, we *assure* freedom to the *free*."[38]

Ralph Waldo Emerson had no doubts that the president would follow through. In an essay published in the *Atlantic Monthly*, he said: "it is not a measure that admits of taking back. Done, it cannot be undone by a new administration." Emerson appreciated what others criticized: "the firm tone in which he announces it, without inflation or surplusage." Lincoln's apparent reticence and moderation were his great strength, a fairness of mind whose "capacity and virtue...we have underestimated." Emerson could hardly wait for the hour to strike. "Do not let the dying die," he implored. "Hold them back to this world, until you have charged their ear and heart with this message to other spiritual societies, announcing the melioration of our planet."[39]

CHAPTER 4

1863

ON JANUARY 1, THOMAS WENTWORTH HIGGINSON ATTENDED services to commemorate the Emancipation Proclamation. Higginson had been one of the secret six that supported John Brown's raid on Harper's Ferry in 1859, and was now serving at Port Royal, South Carolina, as the colonel of the First South Carolina Volunteers, the first black regiment authorized by the federal government during the war. Located in Beaufort County, Port Royal fell into Union hands early in the war and, since then, Northern whites and local blacks had participated in an experiment in free plantation labor.

The proclamation was read and the colors presented. As Higginson saluted the flag,

there suddenly arose, close beside the platform, a strong male voice, (but rather cracked and elderly), into which two women's voices instantly blended, singing, as if by an impulse that could be no more repressed than the morning note of the song-sparrow,-

My Country 'tis of thee,
Sweet land of liberty,
Of thee I sing...!

I never saw anything so electric; it made all other words cheap; it seemed the choked voice of a race at last unloosed.[1]

Lincoln had followed through and issued the Emancipation Proclamation. The final Proclamation included several important changes from the preliminary decree announced one hundred days earlier. It omitted any reference to schemes of colonization. It specified those places that were "this day in rebellion against the United States" and declared that all persons held there as slaves "henceforward shall be free." (The preliminary decree said "forever free," but now that the deed was done, as opposed to promised, the additional rhetoric seemed unnecessary.) The document also included a provision for receiving "persons of suitable condition" into the military. This would prove to be of signal importance in the war effort and for the future of African Americans. At a meeting with his cabinet held December 31, Lincoln added a line, proposed by Salmon Chase, that allowed the legalistic document to breathe: "And upon this act, sincerely believed to be an act of justice, warranted by the Constitution, upon military necessity, I invoke the considerate judgment of mankind, and the gracious favor of almighty God."[2]

The Proclamation elated Northern Republicans, dismayed Northern Democrats, and outraged Southern rebels—Jefferson Davis called it the "most execrable measure recorded in the history of guilty man." The enslaved heard the news that the day of Jubilee had come, and their pace of escape to Union lines increased: "whole families of them are stampeding and leaving their masters," wrote one officer. Many Union soldiers responded with joy that the war was not merely a battle "between North & South; but a contest between human rights and human liberty on the one side and eternal bondage on the other." But others expressed alarm. A surgeon with the Army of the Potomac confessed, "I have no fancy for emancipating a lot of uneducated wild, ferocious, and brutal negroes." Some officers complained to the president about this dramatic shift in military objectives and asked him to revoke the Proclamation. Lincoln responded that "broken eggs can not be mended. I have issued the emancipation proclamation and I cannot retract it. . . . And being made, it must stand."[3]

The Proclamation was one of several actions Lincoln took in January in his effort to advance the Union's military success. On January 4, he ordered General Grant to rescind his Special Order Number 11, which had expelled all Jews as a class from his military department. Henry Halleck, who like Grant evinced hostility to Jewish merchants, said the president opposed proscribing "an entire religious class, some of whom are fighting in our ranks." Later in the month, Lincoln replaced Burnside with Joseph Hooker as commander of the Army of the Potomac. Hooker had graduated from West Point in 1827 and served in the Mexican War. He was ambitious, and after making the appointment Lincoln warned him to "beware of rash-ness." After the defeat at Marye's Heights, the army needed reorganization and a morale boost, and Hooker provided it. Finally, in the west, Grant personally took over the campaign against Vicksburg, Mississippi, which had begun unsuccessfully in December 1862.[4]

The war was taking its toll north and south. Military losses and a short-age of enlistments led Lincoln to sign an Enrollment or Conscription Act on March 3. Male citizens between the ages of twenty and forty-five had to enroll, and quotas for various congressional districts were set to be filled by the states. As with Confederate conscription, the Union draft permitted the hiring of substitutes. On both sides there were also serial volunteers, men who would enlist, receive as much as several hundred dollars in gold, and desert, only to sign up again for another bounty. By midsummer, the draft would lead to violent conflict.

The Confederacy had instituted its draft a year earlier but now found itself suffering from shortages of food and goods. Attempts to convince planters to switch from cotton to food production had limited success. And Southerners bristled at being told by the government not to distill liquor from corn because the grain was needed. Drought in 1862 had destroyed much of the crop in Virginia and elsewhere, and a scarcity of salt, which was used as a preservative, kept army meat rations skimpy. High inflation crippled the economy as the price of wheat and milk tri-pled. Speculators tried to profit off of the situation, and in several cities riots took place in the spring. On April 3, in Richmond, women broke into food and clothing stores, shouting "bread, bread." Only the threat of the militia firing broke up the crowd.

Seeking a solution to the food problem, the Confederate Congress passed a tax-in-kind law on April 24. The tax took 10 percent of all agri-cultural produce and any livestock raised for slaughter. It did little to ease the supply crisis, but it increased tensions within the Confederacy over how the war was being fought and whether its professed principles were being upheld. States' rights ideologues, who believed that the reason for secession was to escape a tyrannical centralized government, were increas-ingly reluctant to comply with the Confederate government's demands, essential though they were to waging war effectively.

The Chancellorsville Campaign of April 30 to May 6 renewed Confederate hopes. After crossing the Rappahannock and Rapidan rivers above Fredericksburg, Hooker's army of 115,000 concentrated near

Chancellorsville. Faced with superior numbers attacking his force of sixty thousand, Lee boldly divided his army. Meeting resistance on the Orange Turnpike, which led to Fredericksburg, Hooker inexplicably halted, assumed defensive positions, and yielded the initiative to Lee, who again divided his forces, sending Stonewall Jackson to attack the Union right flank. They were unprepared for the attack. Hooker never brought his reserve forces into the battle, and after several days the Army of the Potomac retreated. The Union suffered 17,000 casualties compared to 12,800 for the Confederacy. But one of those Confederate casualties was Stonewall Jackson, a man described by Lee as "my right arm," who died eight days later from complications with a wound received in battle. Lee had won a brilliant victory but had failed to follow up. He hardly could, with troops ragged and undernourished, men and horses severely under-supplied. Instead, he would reorganize his army and prepare to invade the North.

When news of the loss reached Washington, Lincoln could not con-tain his despair. "What will the country say! What will the country say!" he cried. At the same time, he faced a political crisis in the Union over what he called "the fire in the rear," the vocal opposition of Northern Peace Democrats to the ongoing prosecution of the war. Dismayed by declara-tions of sympathy for the enemy, General Burnside, commanding the military district of Ohio, issued an order in April that anyone who acted in support of the enemy would be tried as a spy or traitor and executed if convicted.[5]

It didn't take long before Clement Vallandigham tested the order. A former Democratic congressman, Vallandigham had his eye on the governorship of Ohio. When he delivered a speech on May 1 denouncing Lincoln and the war effort, it was not the first time that he had spoken out. On January 14 in an address to the House, "The Great Civil War in America," he had declared that the war should not continue, its cause was not slavery but abolition, and peaceful reunion was still possible. But now, before a crowd of ten thousand in Mt. Vernon, Ohio, he lambasted a "wicked, cruel, and unnecessary war, one not waged for the preserva-tion of the Union, but for the purpose of crushing out liberty and to erect a despotism; a war for the freedom of the blacks and the enslave-ment of the whites."[6]

Vallandigham was arrested for violating Burnside's order. Authorities denied him a writ of habeas corpus and tried him before a military tribunal, which found him guilty and sentenced him to two years' confinement. Lincoln altered the sentence to banishment but upheld his general's orders. A political firestorm erupted. The president, who had only selectively addressed the public directly on state matters, decided to issue a letter in response to a protest from a group of New York Democrats led by Erastus Corning, head of the New York Central Railroad, who condemned the arrest and trial as "a fatal blow" to the liberties guaranteed by the Constitution.

In the missive, Lincoln did not simply declare his position; he walked readers through his logic. "Ours is a case of rebellion," he said, "in fact, a clear, flagrant, and gigantic case of rebellion." The Constitution stated that the writ of habeas corpus shall not be suspended except in "cases of rebellion or invasion." Lincoln said that in this case there was no distinction between areas of military occupation and those not so occupied—the whole nation was at war, and Vallandigham's arrest "was made because he was laboring, with some effect, to prevent the raising of troops; to encourage desertions from the army; and to leave the rebellion without an adequate military force to suppress it." He then asked readers: "must I shoot a simple-minded soldier boy who deserts, while I must not touch the hair of the wily agitator who induces him to desert?" and answered his own question: "I think that in such a case to silence the agitator, and save the boy is not only constitutional, but withal a great mercy." He must have known as well how soldiers felt. One captain wrote to his brother, "My *first* object is to crush this infernal Rebellion the *next* to come North and bayonet such fool miscreants as Vallandigham."[7]

As Lincoln sought to quell the fire in the rear, the fire on the front gathered force. Through the spring, Grant planned and executed an assault on Vicksburg, which sat on a bluff high above the Mississippi on its eastern bank. To take the heavily fortified fortress at Vicksburg would be to control the mighty river, gain access to the lower Confederacy, and cut off the trans-Mississippi Confederacy from the rest of it. Overcoming great obstacles, Grant marched his army south of Vicksburg and sent supporting barges and transports down the river past the Confederate batteries, which fired relentlessly on the flotilla. He then recrossed the river. Living off of the land, Grant's army, now divided, fought its way west and defeated opposing forces at Jackson (May 14), Champion Hill (May 16), and Big Black River (May 17). Grant now had Confederate general John Pemberton's army trapped at Vicksburg. After two brutal frontal assaults failed, Grant settled in for a siege of the city. His men dug miles of trenches and tunnels, some of which reached into Confederate lines. The siege would be a long one, and at times, at night, soldiers from each side gathered to exchange rations and stories. Lincoln called the campaign— whether or not Vicksburg fell—"one of the most brilliant in the world."[8]

As Vicksburg came under siege, another general who had proven to be a brilliant tactician planned a Confederate invasion of the North. Lee's Army of Northern Virginia had eighty thousand men organized into three infantry corps led by James Longstreet, Richard Ewell, and Ambrose Powell Hill. James E. B. Stuart, who had literally run a circle around McClellan's Army of the Potomac a year earlier in the Peninsula campaign, commanded the cavalry. In May, the Confederate cabinet gave approval to Lee's plan, which had several objectives: to relieve pressure on Richmond, to exploit the rich resources of the Pennsylvania countryside, and perhaps, by capturing a major Northern city, to win support for the Confederacy from England. *Harper's Weekly* speculated that Lee's invasion sought to boost Confederate morale in the face of the siege at Vicksburg but thought it could not possibly succeed because "no army the size of Lee's can operate as a moving or flying column without a base."[9]

Lincoln feared that Hooker was not up to the task of confronting Lee. He was frustrated that, like McClellan, the general seemed more focused on Richmond than on Lee's army. He told Gideon Welles that "Hooker may commit the same fault as McClellan and lose his chance." "Almost every one sees," wrote one newspaper correspondent, "that if General Lee gains a decisive victory over Hooker, which he is very likely to do, the cause of the North is virtually lost." On June 28, Hooker offered his resignation; Lincoln appointed George Gordon Meade to command the Army of the Potomac.[10]

Like his predecessor, Meade had graduated from West Point in 1835 and served in the Mexican War. He had also worked as a civil engineer. He had been wounded during the Seven Days' battles but had recovered and had fought at Second Bull Run. Coming so suddenly, the appointment shocked Meade, and he protested against it. He took command just days before the battle against Lee commenced on July 1 when a Confederate brigade encountered Union cavalry along the Chambersburg Pike west of Gettysburg, Pennsylvania. After the first day of fighting, Confederates drove back outnumbered Union forces, who took a position on Cemetery Hill. That evening, the remaining forces on both sides reached Gettysburg—a total of more than 150,000 men (eighty-three thousand Union and seventy-five thousand Confederate).

On July 2, Lee ordered Longstreet to attack the Union left, with a secondary assault on the right led by Ewell. The day saw gruesome combat as Confederates repeatedly attacked and Union forces held their ground. The fighting on the left occurred at Little Round Top, Devil's Den, the Wheat Field, and Peach Orchard and the fighting on the right at Culp's Hill. A few weeks later, a Union soldier wrote: "Bullets whistled past us; shells screeched over us; canister and grape fell about us; comrade after comrade dropped from the ranks; but on the line went. No one took a second look at his fallen companion. We had no time to weep...forward we went again and the Rebs were routed, and the bloody field was in our possession; but at what a cost! The ground was strewed with dead and dying, whose groans and prayers and cries for help and water rent the air. The sun had gone down and in the darkness we hurried, stumbled over the field in search of our fallen companions, and when the living were cared for, laid ourselves down on the ground to gain a little rest, for the morrow bid far more stern and bloody work, the living sleeping side by side with the dead."[11]

On July 3, Lee decided to attack the Union center, embedded along Cemetery Hill. Longstreet thought it would be better to outflank the Union line on the left and maneuver behind them. But Lee was determined to fight. A division of fresh troops led by George Pickett had arrived the night before. In the morning, Union soldiers battled at Culp's Hill and regained what they had lost the day before. At the same time, J. E. B. Stuart's cavalry, which had arrived only the previous day, failed in an attempt to sneak behind Union lines. At one o'clock in the afternoon, Confederate artillery began an intense bombardment of the Union center. For a time, Union artillery responded, but then it stopped, for several reasons: to conserve ammunition, to deceive the Confederates into thinking they had put it out of action, and, as one Union artillerist honestly put it, to endure "dreadful artillery fire [that] seemed to paralyze our whole line for [a] while." After two hours of shelling, the rebels emerged from the woods.[12]

Nine infantry brigades, some 12,500 men, led an assault across three-fourths of a mile of undulating open field toward entrenched Union positions behind a low stone wall. The Confederate line stretched a mile wide, with Pettigrew and Trimble on the left and Pickett on the right. The assault, straight into a "torrent of iron & leaden ball," lasted an hour. When it ended, the Confederate attackers were decimated, having suffered casualties of 50 percent. Thousands were killed, wounded, or captured, with extremely high casualties among officers. A few brave Confederates made it over the stone wall and there ended their journey. Pickett would never get over the destruction of his division, and after the war those generals who hailed from Virginia would cast blame on Longstreet, who was born in South Carolina and had expressed concern about Lee's plan. As Lee sought to gather what was left of his army (he suffered total casualties of over twenty-eight thousand; the Union lost nearly twenty-three thousand) he was heard to say, "It's all my fault." Later, he would blame Longstreet and Stuart. He would also offer a jeremiad, pronouncing "we have sinned against almighty God" and calling for a purging of collective sin to win God back to the Confederate side.[13]

It poured on the evening of July 4. The next day, Union troops renewed their march. One soldier wrote: "Crossing the battlefield—Cemitary Hill—the Great Wheat Field Farm—Seminary ridge—and

Timothy H. O'Sullivan, *A Harvest of Death* (Gettysburg, 1863). Courtesy of Library of Congress.

other places where dead men, horses, smashed artillery, were strewn in utter confusion, the Blue and the Grey Mixed—Their bodies so bloated—distorted—discolored on account of decomposition having set in that they were utterly unrecognizable, save by clothing, or things in their pockets—The scene simply beggars description."[14]

Lee retreated from Gettysburg, but Meade did not counterattack, and his failure to do so enraged Lincoln, especially after rains came and the rising waters of the Potomac prevented Lee from crossing back into Virginia. On July 14, he wrote a letter to Meade: "My dear general, I do not believe you appreciate the magnitude of the misfortune involved in Lee's escape. He was within your easy grasp, and to have closed upon him would, in connection with our other late successes, have ended the war. As it is, the war will be prolonged indefinitely." Lincoln decided not to send the rebuke, using back channels instead to get his message to the general.[15]

One of the other successes Lincoln alluded to was Vicksburg, which, on July 4, surrendered to Grant. Pemberton's force of thirty thousand had been reduced by disease as well as the constant shelling inflicted on the city. The diary of one Mississippi soldier narrated the struggle to survive on quarter rations, weeds, slaughtered mules, and trapped rats. The soldiers sent the commander a petition on June 28: "if you can't feed us, you had better surrender." The siege had lasted forty-six days. Pemberton delivered his men and arms. Grant paroled the soldiers, allowing them to go home after they swore not to take up arms again. He used the captured rifles to reequip his men.[16]

On both sides, commentators recognized the momentousness of the event. Jefferson Davis had said that "Vicksburg is the nail head that [holds] the South's two halves together." If so, the nail had been pulverized. One Confederate wrote, "This is the most terrible blow that has been struck yet." Davis, "in the depth of gloom," confessed "we are now in the darkest hour of our political existence."[17]

Gideon Welles noted in his diary that "the rejoicing in regard to Vicksburg is immense ... [it] has excited a degree of enthusiasm not excelled during the war." Lincoln wrote to Grant, whom he had never met, and thanked him for "the almost inestimable service you have done the country." Sherman wired Grant calling it "the best fourth of July since 1776. Of course we must not rest idle, only don't let us brag too soon."[18]

Sherman was prescient. More good news arrived with word of the surrender of Port Hudson on July 9, which gave complete control of the Mississippi to the Union. But then New York exploded in riots over the draft. On July 11, names were first drawn in New York in compliance with the Conscription Act passed several months earlier. Two days later, another drawing was to be held, but a crowd of several hundred attacked the draft office. Many of the protesters were Irish immigrants, Democrats who had multiple resentments: that the wealthy could buy substitutes for $300, that the war showed no sign of ending, and that they had to compete for jobs with free blacks, whose numbers they believed would only grow with emancipation. The rioters overwhelmed the police and let loose on the black community a wave of horrific racial violence. They burned buildings, including the Colored Orphan Asylum, and lynched more than a dozen blacks, stringing them up from lamp posts. They also sought out the homes of leading Republicans such as Horace Greeley. After two more days of violence, the riots subsided when New York militia regiments arrived to reestablish order. One witness testified afterward: "I believe if I were to live a hundred years I would never forget that scene, or cease to hear the horrid voices of that demoniacal mob resounding in my ears."[19]

Lincoln would not tolerate rebellion against federal authority in the North any more than he tolerated it in the South. He reasserted his intentions to "see the draft law faithfully executed." When New York next held draft selection, twenty thousand troops made certain there was no violence. Ironically, at the moment that racial hatred ignited draft riots, black troops began to make their presence felt in the war effort.

Prior to 1863, selected black units had been organized. Lincoln feared that arming blacks, including those formerly enslaved, would result in the loss of the border states, and he shared many of the prejudices of the day concerning the ability of black men in the field, believing that they would either be too docile or too savage. But all of this changed with the Emancipation Proclamation, which called for accepting blacks into the military. Lincoln came to realize that "the colored population is the great *available* and yet *unavailed* of, force for the restoration of the Union.... The bare sight of fifty thousand armed, and drilled black soldiers on the banks of the Mississippi, would end the rebellion at once."[20]

Lincoln thought of black soldiers primarily as helping to end the war, but recruiters such as Frederick Douglass saw more deeply into the meaning of their service. Only by allowing black men to fight would "the paper proclamation...be made iron, lead and fire." And their service would not only help save the union but also win them citizenship rights: "Once let the black man get upon his person the brass letters, U.S., let

him get an eagle on his button, and a musket on his shoulder and bullets
in his pocket, there is no power on earth that can deny that he has earned
the right to citizenship."[21]

Images as well as words played a role in the recruitment process.
When during the spring a runaway slave appeared in Union lines, a pho-
tographer had him pose with his shirt off. The resulting image shocked
viewers who saw evidence of the barbaric cruelty of slavery; yet the beaten
slave still held his chin up and even defiantly placed his hand on hip.
Entitled "The Scourged Back," or "A Map of Slavery," that photograph
circulated as a carte de visite. One newspaper declared that the "Card
Photograph should be multiplied by the 100,000 and scattered over the
states. It tells the story in a way that even Mrs. Stowe cannot approach
because it tells the story to the eye."

The image also appeared as an engraving in *Harper's Weekly* in its issue
of July 4, 1863. Under the title "A Typical Negro," the weekly told the
man's story. His name was Gordon, and he had entered Union lines at
Baton Rouge, having escaped from his master in Mississippi. During

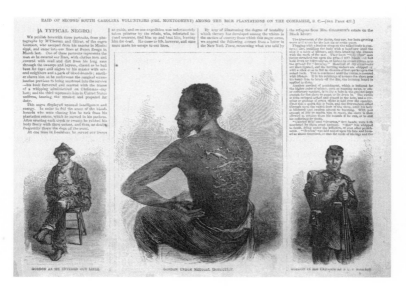

"Gordon as he entered our Lines," Engraving, *Harper's Weekly*, July 4, 1863.
Courtesy of Library of Congress.

his escape, he carried onions to throw dogs off his scent. He arrived tattered and starving, as depicted in the first sketch. The second, drawn from the photograph, shows him undergoing examination before being mustered into the service. And the third "represents him in United States uniform, bearing the musket, and prepared for duty."[22] The images served as an effective recruitment poster.

By war's end, nearly 180,000 men served in the United States Colored Troops, close to 10 percent of the entire Union army. Another nineteen thousand served in the navy. Black soldiers faced myriad difficulties. Though eager to see combat, most of them were initially placed in noncombat situations working on fortifications or as teamsters and cooks. And they suffered the taunts of white soldiers, who enjoyed such pranks as sneaking up on blacks and throwing flour in their faces. Prejudice against them meant not only skepticism about their ability to fight but also harsher punishments and unequal treatment. They served in segregated units commanded by white officers and received less pay than white soldiers—$10 per month with $3 deducted for clothing, compared to $13 plus a clothing allowance for white soldiers; one outraged black corporal wrote directly to the president and declared, "we have done a Soldier's duty. Why can't we have a Soldier's pay?" Finally, captured black soldiers faced a Confederate threat of being returned to slavery, a threat that led Lincoln to issue a general order that announced there would be reprisal against any Confederate prisoners should black troops or their white officers face mistreatment.[23]

In combat, when the chance came, black troops proved their valor and won over skeptics. They played an important role at Port Hudson and Milliken's Bend in the Vicksburg Campaign (one soldier wrote, "the problem of whether the Negroes will fight or not has been solved"). Their performance on July 18 at Fort Wagner, south of Charleston Harbor, where the Massachusetts Fifty-fourth under Colonel Robert Gould Shaw led the assault, forever earned them respect. Shaw was killed, as were scores of his men. He was buried with them in a pit. One bitter Massachusetts officer, blaming Shaw's death on his troops, groused, "niggers won't fight as they ought." But a soldier from Ohio expressed a more widespread and growing belief: "there is not a Negro in the army that is not a better man than a rebel, and for whom I have not a thousand times more respect than I have for a traitor." Arming blacks, General Grant declared, was "the heaviest blow yet given the Confederacy."[24]

Lincoln grew tired of hearing from supporters of the Union still upset by the Emancipation Proclamation and other administration policies. In August, he used an invitation from his friend James Conkling to write a letter to be delivered at a Union rally in Illinois, held on September 3. Conkling had the missive read to the crowd of fifty thousand there, and it was later published in newspapers throughout the Union.

Lincoln defended the Proclamation, saying that "as law, [it] either is valid, or is not valid. If it is not valid, it needs no retraction. If it is valid, it can not be retracted any more than the dead can be brought to life." He went further: "Some say you will not fight to free negroes. Some of them seem willing to fight for you; but, no matter. Fight you, then, exclusively to save the Union." He expressed hope, in the aftermath of Gettysburg and Vicksburg, that peace might come soon. When that day arrived, he said, "there will be some black men who can remember that, with silent tongue, and clenched teeth, and steady eye, and well-poised bayonet, they have helped mankind on to this great consummation; while, I fear, there will be some white ones, unable to forget with malignant heart, and deceitful speech, they have strove to hinder it."[25]

The speech electrified readers, united supporters, and perhaps even converted a few critics. The *New York Times* named Lincoln a "leader who is peculiarly adapted to the needs of the time." The *Chicago Tribune* called it "one of those remarkably clear and forcible documents that come only from Mr. Lincoln's pen....God bless Old Abe."[26]

And yet the war showed no signs of relenting. A border war between Kansas and Missouri turned savage on August 21, when William Quantrill, leader of a pro-Confederate guerilla band, raided Lawrence, Kansas, and murdered some two hundred men and boys and burned down buildings. "The citizens were massacred by the light of their burning homes, and their bodies flung into wells and cisterns," reported one paper. "No other instance of such wanton brutality has occurred during the American war."

In September, a year after Antietam, Union forces under William Rosecrans's Army of the Cumberland engaged in a brutal battle with Braxton Bragg's Army of Tennessee at Chickamauga, Georgia. Earlier in the year, in June, Rosecrans had managed dramatic success against Bragg when he took Chattanooga, but his accomplishment went almost unacknowledged in the Union successes at Vicksburg and Gettysburg. Now, Bragg had Longstreet, who arrived from Virginia in time to break through Union lines and drive them back to Chattanooga. Combined casualties were nearly 35,000 out of some 120,000 engaged. The victory provided the Confederacy with a morale boost. "The whole South will be filled again with patriotic fervor," noted a Richmond resident. Writing to his brother, Henry Adams predicted that the loss "ensures us another year of war."[27]

Two months later, fortunes would be reversed at Missionary Ridge, which stretched southeast from Chattanooga. In October, Lincoln had placed Grant in charge of the entire western military department. Grant traveled to Chattanooga to oversee operations in the Tennessee theater. Bragg was dug in atop the seemingly impregnable four-hundred-foot ridge. And yet on November 25, Union forces charged up the ridge and drove the rebels from their position, routing Bragg and his army. The next day, a civilian clerk wrote, "it would seem incredible to one who had not seen it, to think that men could climb up such a hill, in face of the fire they were receiving, and not only get up the hill, but, actually drive a force, superior in numbers off of it." The Union now held Chattanooga, the "Gateway to the Lower South." For the most part, the remainder of the year was quiet as both armies settled into winter quarters, waiting for the spring to resume warfare.[28]

On November 19, days before the success at Missionary Ridge, Lincoln visited the site of the summer's momentous Union victory at Gettysburg to participate in ceremonies dedicating the Soldiers National Cemetery. The main speaker was Edward Everett, former governor and senator from Massachusetts, whose oration went on for two hours. Following a hymn, Lincoln offered his remarks, approximately 272 words, though the total varies with a word here, a word there, in the five known manuscript copies of the address.

The speech's rhetoric was historical and biblical, as Lincoln grounded the meaning of the war in what took place in 1776 (four score and seven years earlier) and defined what had taken place then as the creation of a nation devoted to liberty and equality. The cadences are musical, the rule of threes doing its work effectively: "we cannot consecrate, we cannot dedicate, we cannot hallow this ground"; "of the people, by the people, for the people." Lincoln separated words from actions, knowing that in war the latter were the coin of victory, and yet words helped give meaning to deeds.

Lincoln's opponents were livid. They saw what he had done: he had hijacked the meaning of the nation in such a way as to make liberty and equality central to its identity, and he had taken the events of the year—from emancipation through Gettysburg and Vicksburg and through the enlistment of black troops—to define what this "great civil war" was about: not simply restoring the Union but creating a better nation dedicated to making palpable the principles of the revolution. A Democratic newspaper called it "a perversion of history so flagrant that the most extended charity cannot regard it as otherwise than willful."[29]

Lincoln was already contemplating the end of the war and how the nation would be reconstituted. It was a question he was not alone in considering. More than a year earlier, one soldier wondered in his diary: "What shall we do with the conquered country? With the slaves? With meddlesome foreigners? With our vast debt? With the rebels themselves?" On December 8, the president issued a "Proclamation of Amnesty and Reconstruction." Lincoln offered a full pardon to participants in the rebellion (except government officials, high-ranking officers, and those rebels who had mistreated prisoners of war) who took an oath of allegiance, with property restored to them save for slaves. Furthermore, whenever 10 percent of those who voted in a state in the election of 1860 took the oath, state government could be reestablished and would be recognized. He also declared he would not object to provisions established to aid former slaves, "a laboring, landless, and homeless class" of people.[30]

The proclamation initially pleased both radical and conservative elements within the Republican Party. It was a first attempt to look beyond the war to the terms of reconstruction—the ways the divided nation would be restored to one. The proclamation also seemed to play to a growing peace movement within the Confederacy, as representatives hostile to Jefferson Davis gained seats in the fall elections and North Carolina expressed interest in opening separate peace negotiations. But the process of reconstruction was still a long way off. Late in the year, both sides began to strategize over the presidential election scheduled for 1864. In a war that had not been going well for the Confederacy, the defeat of Lincoln might still salvage the rebels' cause. Entering the year, Lincoln was uncertain about his chances. There was not only much war weariness and opposition from Northern Democrats but also dissent from radical and conservative Republicans. The nation was not yet ready for reconstruction, not by a long shot.

CHAPTER 5

1864

IN DECEMBER 1863, SALMON CHASE SUGGESTED ADDING
the phrase "In God We Trust" to American coins, and with the Coinage
Act of 1864 Congress approved the motto. Both sides believed that God
supported their cause, and soldiers often expressed a deep religious
faith, at least in combat. "If ever one needed God's help," wrote a Georgia
private, "it is in time of battle." Though the embrace of religion seldom
showed in attendance at Sunday services in camp, one soldier observed
that "still there is large amt of a certain kind of rude religious feeling."
Through 1864, Confederate soldiers in particular experienced revivals
of religion. They held prayer meetings and used faith to spur courage.
But at the start of the year, problems within the Confederacy were taking
their toll. One North Carolinian wrote to the governor, "The tide is
against us, everything is against us. I fear the God who rules the destinies
of nations is against us."[1]

With the effects of the blockade taking hold, and ill-advised fiscal policies that relied heavily on paper money to finance the war, inflation
began to wreck havoc. Planters had failed to shift from cotton to staples,
and transportation networks, such as they were, had been disrupted.
One diarist listed prices in Richmond as $275 a barrel for flour; $25 a
bushel for potatoes; $9 a pound for bacon. A pair of shoes could cost
over $100. In 1860, a typical Southerner spent $6.55 to feed a family for
a week; by 1864 the amount had ballooned to $68.25 for the same sta-
ples. Women especially, held up in Southern culture as refined and pure,
carried the burden and suffered from want and fear, especially in situa-

tions where they were left alone to manage slaves. Perhaps as many as one in ten Confederate soldiers deserted, many to return to help their families. A revised Conscription Act passed in February made men aged seventeen to fifty susceptible to the draft. "We want this war stopped," wrote one man. "We will take peace on *any terms* that are *honorable.*"[2]

Jefferson Davis faced not only an unraveling economic situation, but a difficult political one as well. More extreme political elements in the government, such as Barnwell Rhett and William Yancey, had little respect for the Confederate president. Davis had cobbled together his cabinet to appease the interests of individual states rather than bring the best people into government. Rather than lubricating the engine of government, one-party politics actually made it more difficult for Davis to act as a strong executive because a constantly changing constellation of interests pulled and pushed in different directions; by comparison, in the Union, the existence of the Democrats helped unify the Republicans in support behind Lincoln. Davis enjoyed no such support. Indeed, many an antiadministration official came to feel about Davis as did the editor of the *Southern Literary Messenger,* who called him "cold, haughty, peevish, narrow-minded, pig-headed, *malignant.*" And the tension between the doctrine of states' rights and the need for national actions continued to impede the Confederate war effort as governors resisted Davis's call for men and material.[3]

Despite being ridiculed as "no military genius," Davis inserted himself directly into military affairs and throughout the spring consulted with Lee about operations. They were especially concerned about what Grant might do. On March 1, Lincoln nominated Grant to command all armies, and on March 9, a day after meeting him for the first time, Lincoln placed him in charge. Grant made his headquarters the Army of the Potomac, located where Union forces would be going head-to-head against Lee. But where they would tangle remained uncertain. On March 25, Lee wrote to Davis and warned him of falling prey to reports in Northern newspapers as to Union military intentions. "I would advise," Lee wrote, "that we make the best preparations in our power to meet an advance in any quarter, but be careful not to suffer ourselves to be misled by feigned movements into strengthening one point at the expense of others, equally exposed and equally important."[4]

Grant's strategy was for Meade's Army of the Potomac (one hundred fifteen thousand men) to move against Lee's Army of Northern Virginia (sixty-five thousand men). Auxiliary attacks would include action on the

James River and in the Shenandoah Valley. In addition, Sherman (with one hundred thousand men), who now assumed Grant's old command, would focus on Georgia, where he faced Joseph Johnston (with sixty-five thousand troops). Nathaniel Banks would lead a campaign in Louisiana on the Red River. But these auxiliary campaigns in March, April, and May came to nothing. Grant would go to Virginia and face Lee without the help these actions, had they been successful, would have provided.

Whatever impact Union losses in peripheral battles such as Olustee in Florida, Poison Springs in Arkansas, and Fort Pillow in Tennessee had on Northern morale, reports of atrocities committed by rebels against black troops in these engagements shocked the North. At Fort Pillow, on April 12, forces under Confederate general Nathan Bedford Forrest murdered dozens of men after they surrendered. In his report three days later, Forrest wrote, "the river was dyed with the blood of the slaughtered for two hundred yards." Lincoln rejected outright retaliation, but the administration continued to refuse any exchange of prisoners unless black soldiers received equal treatment. And Union soldiers found ways to retaliate. After a battle in Mississippi, a lieutenant wrote, "We did not take many prisoners. The Negroes remembered 'Fort Pillow.'"[5]

The prisoners-of-war issue became especially controversial when Northerners learned of the abhorrent conditions at Andersonville Prison in Georgia. Opened in February, by the summer the camp population swelled to over thirty thousand. Men had no shelter, very little food, and water only from a polluted stream. The soldiers, one Union prisoner wrote, were "walking skeletons, covered with filth and vermin." Thousands died from disease and malnutrition. One soldier who kept a diary wrote on August 22 that "the men dys verry fast hear now from 75 to 125 per day." After the war, Henry Wirz, a Confederate commander in charge of the prison, was tried for murder and executed. Through the spring, the Confederates continued to refuse equal treatment of black soldiers, and Grant became convinced that as Confederate forces diminished in strength it might be best not to exchange rebels, who would in all likelihood only return to the fight. By war's end, 194,000 Union and 215,000 Confederate soldiers had been held as prisoners, resulting in thirty thousand Union and twenty-six thousand Confederate deaths.[6]

Grant hoped his Virginia offensive, known as the Overland Campaign, would take many more prisoners. On May 5–7, the first battle took place at the Wilderness, some seventy square miles of forested terrain in central

Virginia. During two days of brutal warfare in dense woods, Union forces suffered nearly eighteen thousand casualties and the Confederates eleven thousand. Had Grant withdrawn, it would have been a Confederate victory. Instead it was a tactical draw, with Grant determined still to push onto Richmond. On May 11, he informed Lincoln: "I propose to fight it out on this line if it takes all summer."[7]

The telegram came in the midst of fighting at Spotsylvania Courthouse. Lee had time to build up his defenses with logs and earthworks. The fight, which pulsated over two weeks, included a span of twenty-two hours where the forces engaged in hand-to-hand combat at a location called the "Bloody Angle." Bodies piled several deep filled the trenches, and men shot and stabbed one another both through and over the fortifications. The rifle fire was so furious that it felled a sturdy oak tree. One Confederate called it "a Golgotha of horrors." In the end, the Union suffered eighteen thousand casualties and Confederates twelve thousand. But Grant simply disengaged and continued his attempt to outflank Lee and threaten Richmond.[8]

Grant's Overland Campaign culminated on June 3, when he ordered a frontal assault at Cold Harbor against Lee's well-fortified men. Union soldiers, who had survived Spotsylvania, knew what to expect. Some pinned their names to their uniforms so that their bodies could be identified afterward. They never made it to the entrenchments. In an hour, seven thousand were killed or wounded, compared to fifteen hundred rebels. Fighting would continue sporadically for a few more days, but Grant gave up on taking Richmond directly and now set his sights on Petersburg, a crucial rail junction south of the capital. In two months, the Army of the Potomac had lost almost two-thirds the number of men it had lost in the previous three years combined. Following days of operating on the wounded, John G. Perry, a Union surgeon, exclaimed "War! War! War! I often think that in the future, when human character shall have deepened, there will be a better way of settling affairs than this of plunging into a perfect maelstrom of horror."[9]

The defeat at Cold Harbor came at a politically precarious time for Lincoln. Any number of rivals, including his own secretary of the treasury, Salmon P. Chase, were angling for the Republican presidential nomination in 1864 (the party called itself the National Union Party to make clear its purpose). A bitter John C. Fremont, the Republican candidate in 1856, aggrieved over having been relieved of his command, emerged as the candidate of a group of radical Republicans. Other names surfaced, including Benjamin Butler. Some mentioned Grant as a candidate. In addition to the factionalism within the Republican Party, Lincoln had to worry about the Peace Democrats and keeping the support of so-called War Democrats, who favored seeing the contest through to its end. This was no easy task. Democrats in general, whether for continuing to prosecute the war or demanding immediate peace, constituted a significant percentage of voters in the North. In the election of 1860, counting only those states that remained in the Union, Lincoln won 47.2 percent of the votes and the two Democratic candidates 46.6 percent.

While some nationally prominent Republicans may have challenged Lincoln, governors and others attuned to grassroots sentiment successfully promoted him as the people's choice. At the national convention held in Baltimore from June 7–8, delegates unanimously renominated the President. On hearing the news, he said, "I will neither conceal my gratification, nor restrain the expression of my gratitude, that the Union people, through their convention...have deemed me not unworthy to remain in my present position." The platform approved of the government's refusal "to compromise with rebels, or to offer them any terms of peace, except such as may be based upon an unconditional surrender," and at Lincoln's behest, endorsed a constitutional amendment that "shall terminate and forever prohibit the existence of slavery within the limits of the jurisdiction of the United States."[10]

Such an amendment, the Thirteenth, was already in the works. On January 8, the first of several proposals came forward, and the Senate Judiciary Committee resolved differences in language to present an amendment that stated "neither slavery nor involuntary servitude" shall exist in the United States. On April 8, the Senate passed the measure, by a vote of thirty-eight to six. The House voted twice but failed in February and again in June to muster the necessary two-thirds majority. Passage of the amendment would have to wait until after the presidential election.

Whereas Lincoln's emancipation policies faced opposition from both War and Peace Democrats in Congress, his reconstruction policies were challenged by radical Republicans. On July 2, Congress hastily passed the Wade-Davis Bill. Sponsored by Senator Benjamin Wade of Ohio and Representative Henry Winter Davis of Maryland, the bill offered a more stringent approach to reconstruction than the president's. Under its terms, 50 percent of the eligible voters had to take an oath of allegiance; only those who could take an "iron-clad oath" that they had never sup- ported the rebellion would be enfranchised; and a constitutional convention would have to be held before state officials could be elected. Lincoln pocket vetoed the measure. He refused to be "inflexibly commit- ted to any single plan of restoration," not to mention one that differed from his own, and he would not repudiate the progress already made by Arkansas and Louisiana under the presidential plan of reconstruction.

Furthermore, he refused to "declare a constitutional competency in Congress to abolish slavery in States"; on this he had been consistent throughout. Instead, he hoped for eventual passage of a constitutional amendment. On August 5, Wade and Davis issued a manifesto in response to Lincoln's veto: "a more studied outrage on the legislative authority of the people has never been perpetrated," they averred.[11]

Through the summer, Union efforts in the war went little better than they had in the spring, leaving Lincoln even more vulnerable politically. On June 18, the Army of the Potomac lost an opportunity to take Petersburg when Lee managed to reinforce his entrenched position. Union forces suffered eight thousand casualties and settled in for a siege of the city. Weeks later, they filled a mine shaft they dug beneath Confederate defenses and exploded it, creating a huge crater. But in the ensuing battle the Union corps under Burnside was beaten back. The siege of Petersburg would continue.

Matters fared no better in the lower South, where Sherman had begun his Atlanta campaign, in which he would face off against Joseph E. Johnston and his Army of the Tennessee. Before it was over, at least nine separate battles would be fought in addition to countless skirmishes. But at places such as New Hope Church and Pickett's Mills in May, and Kennesaw Mountain in June, Confederate forces repulsed Sherman's army. The frontal assaults that so devastated the Army of the Potomac had the same effect on the military division of the Mississippi.

Despite these successes, Confederate leaders grew unhappy with Johnston, who seemed, like McClellan, not to want to fight. On July 17, Davis relieved him of command and replaced him with John Bell Hood. Only thirty-three years old, Hood was wounded at Gettysburg, where he was beaten at Little Round Top. In September, another wound led to the amputation of his right leg. It would fall to the aggressive Hood, who had to be strapped into his saddle, to defend Atlanta.

In the heat of the summer, it seemed as if the war was stalemated. A year had passed since Gettysburg and Vicksburg, and still the Confederates—undermanned, undernourished, undersupplied—fought on, and not just defensively. In early July, Confederate infantry and cavalry under Jubal Early crossed the Potomac for a raid on Washington itself. He reached the outer fortifications of the capital, defended by additional troops hastily recalled from Meade's army. Although Early had to retreat to Virginia, at the end of July his cavalry burned the town of Chambersburg, Pennsylvania, where residents refused to pay a $100,000 ransom.

These developments further depressed morale in the North and gave sustenance to the peace movement, which called for an end to the war under conditions to be negotiated. "What a difference between now and last year!" wrote a visitor to Philadelphia, "No signs of any enthusiasm, no flags; most of the best men gloomy and despairing." Even Horace Greeley joined the chorus, declaring, "our bleeding, bankrupt, almost dying country also longs for peace." Lincoln tried to maintain a public face of good cheer and abiding faith, but in July one visitor described him as "quite paralyzed and wilted down." One critic said, "he does not act or talk or feel like the ruler of a great empire in a great crisis.... He is an unutterable calamity to us where he is." Lincoln came to believe that he would lose the election in November. On August 23 he prepared a memorandum that he asked his cabinet to sign without reading. It stated: "this morning, and for some days past, it seems exceedingly probable that this Administration will not be re-elected. Then it will be my duty to co-operate with the President elect, as to save the Union between the election and the inauguration; as he will have secured his election on such ground that he can not possibly save it afterwards."[12]

Several days later, the Democrats meeting in Chicago nominated McClellan for president. Since being removed by Lincoln in November 1862, he had lived in New Jersey, writing reports defending his military service and making contact with Democratic leaders. His opposition to Lincoln on issues of emancipation and states' rights remained as vociferous as ever. In his letter of acceptance, McClellan declared that "the preservation of our union was the sole avowed object for which the war commenced. It should have been conducted for that object only.... The Union is the one condition of peace—we ask no more." The party platform, however, written in part by no less than Clement Vallandigham, placed peace before union, proclaimed the war a failure, and suggested that after hostilities were halted a "Convention of States" would determine the basis of the "Federal Union of the States." McClellan was a War Democrat forced to run on a peace platform, a combination that could prove untenable.[13]

Republicans such as Gerrit Smith, a founder of the Liberty Party, a social activist and philanthropist, and one of the secret six who had supported John Brown, denounced McClellan's nomination. Calling the Democratic Party "neither more nor less than the Northern wing of the rebellion," he ridiculed McClellan's "pathetic appeal for the votes of soldiers and sailors. What an impudent affectation in him to profess regard for these brave and devoted men, whilst he worms his way up to the platform in which the cause they are battling, bleeding and dying for is condemned and its abandonment called for."[14]

That appeal worried Lincoln and the Republicans, who knew how loyal the men were to the chivalrous McClellan ("no general could ask for greater love and more unbounded confidence than he receives from his men," wrote one officer) and feared the soldiers' vote in the field (eighteen states allowed it, out of which twelve counted the vote separately; only Illinois, Indiana, and New Jersey forbade it) might help swing the election McClellan's way. Fall was approaching, and the Union needed something to help turn momentum its way.[15]

It arrived on September 3 in the form of a telegram from Sherman: "Atlanta is ours, and fairly won." In a campaign that began in May, Sherman's men had fought multiple battles around Atlanta from July onward. The Union commander's strategy was to cut off Hood's supply lines, but repeated attempts failed. Starting on July 20, for weeks, Sherman's artillery bombarded the city, much of whose population of twelve thousand had fled. "I doubt if General Hood will stand a bombardment," wired Sherman on July 21, but stand it he did. Sherman intensified the effort, bringing in from Chattanooga eight large siege guns. Sherman intended to "make the inside of Atlanta too hot to be endured." Finally, in late August, Sherman moved against Hood's railroad supply lines. One of his soldiers explained the general's tenacity this way: "Sherman dont know the word Cant." When Confederate soldiers failed to stop the Union forces at Jonesborough, Hood had no choice but to evacuate Atlanta.[16]

The news that Atlanta had fallen revived Northern morale and Lincoln's chances for reelection. The *Chicago Tribune* declared, "The dark days are over. We see our way out." The *New York Times* said that "the skies begin to brighten.... The clouds that lowered over the Union cause a month ago are breaking away.... The public temper is buoyant and hopeful." George Templeton Strong, in his diary, effused, "Glorious news this morning—*Atlanta taken at last.*"[17]

The fall of Atlanta brought to Confederates a reality they did not want to face. The *Richmond Enquirer* called it a "stunning blow." A North Carolina planter confessed, "never until now did I feel hopeless," and a soldier in Lee's army wrote, "I am afraid that the fall of Atlanta will secure Lincoln's re-election."[18]

In addition to news of Atlanta's capture, Lincoln had received word that Admiral Farragut had managed to overcome heavy fire from two forts and dodge a minefield and sail into Mobile Bay, giving the Union control of the waterway and isolating Mobile. Lincoln was so overjoyed by the double-shot of Mobile and Atlanta that, on September 3, he issued a Proclamation of Prayer and Thanksgiving. He called for "devout acknowledgement to the Supreme Being in whose hands are the destinies of nations" and set aside the following Sunday for thanksgiving to be "offered to Him for His mercy in preserving our national existence against the insurgent rebels who so long have been waging a cruel war against the Government of the United States, for its overthrow."

More success for the Union cause came in September and October, with Philip Sheridan's campaign through the Shenandoah Valley. Embarrassed by Jubal Early's raid on Washington, Grant created the Army of the Shenandoah and put Sheridan in command. He won a stirring victory on September 19 at Opequon Creek and another at Fisher's Hill three days later. On October 19, after Jubal Early surprised the Union at Cedar Creek, Sheridan launched a counterattack that almost destroyed the Confederate army in the area. Union command had learned that the war was as much about resources as men, and just as cutting supply lines in Atlanta had led to victory, so now Sheridan wreaked havoc on the rich farmland of the valley that sustained Lee's army. He reported, "I have destroyed over 2,000 barns filled with wheat, hay, and farming implements; over seventy mills filled with flour and wheat; have driven in front of the army over 4,000 head of stock, and have killed and issued to the troops no less than 3,000 sheep." He said he would leave the valley "with little in it for man or beast." Mary Chesnut, the wife of former South Carolina senator James Chesnut and an inveterate diarist, spoke for many

Southerners when she wrote, on hearing news of Sheridan's exploits, "these stories of our defeats in the valley fall like blows upon a dead body. Since Atlanta I have felt as if all were dead within me."[19]

More good news came Lincoln's way. Not only were military actions succeeding but political initiatives as well. In September, Louisiana, in response to Lincoln's plan for reconstruction, adopted a new state constitution and abolished slavery. Maryland followed suit, its voters approving a new constitution on October 13, to take effect November 1. And three new states had been added to the Union—Kansas in 1861, West Virginia in 1863, and Nevada in 1864, states that would add to his electoral total. Early returns from state elections also boded well: it seemed that Republicans were winning and that the earlier momentum of Democrats calling for peace had been staunched.

The election campaign through the fall turned nasty. Opponents attacked Lincoln personally and suggested that if he was reelected blacks

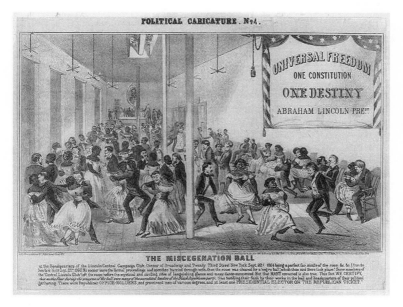

Political Caricature No. 4: The Miscegenation Ball (1864). Courtesy of Library of Congress.

and whites would mingle freely across the nation. A new word was coined, *miscegenation,* to describe a supposed mixing of the races that would necessarily follow a Republican victory. One political caricature, titled "The Miscegenation Ball," showed interracial couples dancing and talking in a hall with a portrait of Lincoln and a banner reading "Universal Freedom. One Constitution. One Destiny. Abraham Lincoln PRE!!!"

Democratic race-baiting failed to carry the Northern electorate. On November 8, the nation learned that Lincoln had been reelected by an overwhelming margin. He won 55 percent of the popular vote. In the electoral college, he took 212 votes and carried 23 states. McClellan won twenty-one electoral votes and three states: New Jersey, Maryland, and Kentucky. The soldier vote also went overwhelmingly for Lincoln. He won at least 78 percent of the votes that were separately counted. One soldier, from the Eleventh Iowa Infantry, reported "our regiment is strong for Old Abraham—three hundred and fourteen votes for Lincoln and forty-two for McClellan"—these men were not about to vote against continuation of the war and the honor of their fallen comrades. The president would continue in office come March, but with a new vice president, Andrew Johnson, a prominent war Democrat who had been serving as military governor of Tennessee since March 1862.[20]

On November 10, Lincoln stood before a crowd that had come to serenade him. Now that it was over, he said that the election, even with all the strife, "has done good too. It has demonstrated that a people's government can sustain a national election, in the midst of a great civil war. Until now it has not been known to the world that this was a possibility.... We can not have free government without elections; and if the rebellion could force us to forego, or postpone a national election, it might fairly claim to have already conquered and ruined us."[21]

Elation among Lincoln's supporters reached unprecedented heights. Diarist George Templeton Strong declared, "the crisis has been past [*sic*], and the most momentous popular election ever held since ballots were invented has decided against treason and disunion." A sergeant in the 120th New York, who had lost a son and a brother-in-law, proclaimed the election "a grand moral victory gained over the combined forces of slavery, disunion, treason, tyranny." And Charles Francis Adams, Jr., in the Union cavalry, wrote to his brother in London, "this election has relieved us of the fire in the rear and now we can devote an undivided attention to the remnants of the Confederacy."[22]

Those remnants tried publicly to put on a brave face. The *Richmond Examiner* said, "the Yankee nation has committed itself to the game of all or nothing; and so must we." But they couldn't fail to notice how peaceably even Lincoln's staunchest opponents reacted to the election. Grant wired "no bloodshed or rioit [*sic*] throughout the land." Lee had warned Davis in September that "our ranks are constantly diminishing by battle and disease, and few recruits are received; the consequences are inevitable." And now the ranks thinned even further with desertion and a sense of hopelessness filtering in. Women wrote asking their husbands and sons to come home, and many of them complied, knowing how severely the war effort had transformed the lives of mothers and daughters who had been forced to take over the responsibilities of running plantations and farms. On November 18, a dispatch from Lee read "desertion is increasing in the army despite all my efforts to stop it."[23]

Despite the devastating losses, Davis and Lee remained resolute. Lincoln informed Congress in his annual message of December 6: "the war continues." He added that "the most remarkable feature in the military operation of the year is General Sherman's attempted march of three hundred miles directly through the insurgent region." He left Atlanta on November 15 with sixty-two thousand men for a 285-mile trek to the seaport city of Savannah. His aim was not so much to engage in combat as to destroy resources and sap the will of a hostile people. "We cannot change the hearts of those people in the South," he said, "but we can make war so terrible...[and] make them so sick of war that generations would pass away before they would again appeal to it." Sherman divided his army into three columns and told Grant that he would "make Georgia howl."[24]

Sherman's army cut a sixty-mile swath across Georgia. On leaving Atlanta, they set a fire that ended up destroying one-third of the city, and they kept up the burning as they marched toward the sea. Sherman's official orders called for widespread foraging, destruction of mills and cotton gins, confiscation of all animals, and the liberation of any able-bodied slaves who could be of service. He explicitly ordered that "soldiers must not enter the dwellings of the inhabitants, or commit any trespass," but those orders often went disobeyed as stragglers unattached to the army wrecked havoc. One soldier recalled, "we had a gay old campaign....Destroyed all we could not eat, stole their niggers, burned their cotton & gins, spilled their sorghum, burned & twisted their R. Roads and raised hell generally."[25]

On December 21, Sherman captured Savannah, a week after a detachment of the Union Army of the Tennessee destroyed what was left of John Bell Hood's forces in a battle at Nashville. Sherman wired Lincoln that he had a present for him, to which the president responded, "many, many thanks for your Christmas gift—the capture of Savannah."[26]

On Christmas Eve, Sherman wrote to Henry Halleck: "We are not only fighting armies, but a hostile people, and must make old and young, rich and poor, feel the hard hand of war, as well as their organized armies. I know that this recent movement of mine through Georgia has had a wonderful effect in this respect. Thousands who had been deceived by their lying papers into the belief that we were being whipped all the time, realized the truth, and have no appetite for a repetition of the same experience."[27]

Earlier in the spring, Jefferson Davis tried as best he could to arouse the Confederate nation against the remorseless war brought to their land: "plunder and devastation of the property of non-combatants, destruction of private dwellings and even of edifices devoted to the worship of God, expeditions organized for the sole purpose of sacking cities, consigning them to flames, killing the unarmed inhabitants and inflicting horrible outrages on women and children are some of the constantly recurring atrocities of the invader." This was before Atlanta and before Sherman's march. Davis could do little but watch the Confederate armies continue to melt away ("two-thirds of our men are absent," he wrote).[28]

Wars begin in an instant, but they conclude slowly. The end would take a few more months, and in those months more lives would be lost. But both sides now sensed it was nearly over.

CHAPTER 6

1865 AND AFTER THE WAR

ON JANUARY 11, 1865, ROBERT E. LEE WROTE A LETTER THAT would have been unthinkable three years earlier. He began by asserting the slaveholder's common view that the relationship between master and slave was "controlled by humane laws and influenced by Christianity and an enlightened public sentiment." He did not want to disturb that relationship, but the course of the war required that the Confederate Congress consider recruiting slaves as soldiers. Lee pointed out that the Union already was using slaves against them, leading in time to a destruction of the institution anyhow. "We must decide," he concluded, "whether slavery will be extinguished by our enemies and the slaves be used against us, or use them ourselves at the risk of the effects which must be produced upon our social institutions. My opinion is that we should employ them without delay." He knew that a promise of freedom would have to accompany enlistment, and he was willing to make it so as to prolong the war.[1]

The idea of slaves fighting for the Confederacy had been broached previously, but always rejected. Most Southerners agreed with Howell Cobb, former congressman from Georgia and a leading Confederate, who argued: "you cannot make soldiers of slaves or slaves of soldiers. The day you make a soldier of them is the beginning of the end of the Revolution. And if slaves will make good soldiers, [then] our whole theory of slavery is wrong." Lee, in his letter, tried to offset this belief, arguing that slaves "can be made efficient soldiers." But decades of pro-slavery ideology that insisted that slaves were docile and happy-go-lucky could not be overturned in a season.[2]

The war compelled Southern women, as well as men, to reconsider their attitudes toward slavery they relied on yet at times also deprecated. Typical of the intellectual gyrations of aristocratic planters, one Georgia belle confessed, "I have sometimes doubted on the subject of slavery. I have seen so many of its evils chief among which is the terribly demoralizing influence upon our men and boys but of late I have become convinced the Negro *as a race* is better off with us as he has been than if he were made free, but I am by no means so sure that we would not gain by his having his freedom given to him." As for arming slaves, she thought it "strangely inconsistent" to offer emancipation to blacks who fought "to aid us in keeping in bondage a large portion of his brethren," whereas "by joining the Yankees he will instantly gain the very reward" of freedom.[3]

Nonetheless, on March 13, Davis signed a bill that allowed for the enlistment of slaves. That the Confederate Congress passed such an act, however narrowly, speaks perhaps to the strength of Confederate nationalism, to a desire to establish an independent Confederacy even without the very institution, slavery, that these states had left the Union to protect in the first place. Thomas Goree, Longstreet's aide-de-camp, put the matter this way: "We had better free the negroes to gain our independence than be subjugated and lose slaves, liberty, and all that makes life dear."[4]

By the time the Confederacy acted on this issue, the Union had done something more direct and complete to assure the abolition of slavery. With the reelection of Lincoln as a mandate, on January 31 the House passed the Thirteenth Amendment by a vote of 119 to 56, only two votes over the two-thirds needed. Lincoln personally involved himself in the legislative process, believing its passage "will bring the war, I have no doubt, rapidly to a close." Before the amendment was submitted to the states for ratification, Lincoln signed it, even though constitutionally he did not have to. In the meantime, both Missouri and Tennessee adopted new state constitutions that abolished slavery.[5]

Few were yet thinking about the contours of postemancipation life for Southern blacks when Sherman, on January 16, issued Special Field Order Number 15, which provided that "the islands from Charleston south, the abandoned rice-fields along the rivers for thirty miles back from the sea, and the country bordering the St. John's River, Florida, are reserved and set apart for the settlement of the negroes now made free by the acts of war and the proclamation of the President of the United

States." Each black family was promised up to forty acres of tillable land. Sherman's order led to the settlement of some forty thousand blacks on confiscated and redistributed land. But by year's end, a new president would revoke the order as reconstruction policy began taking shape.[6]

Whereas Sherman acted alone with Lincoln's permission, Congress took its first steps toward thinking about the former slaves when, on March 3, it passed the bill that created the Bureau of Refugees, Freedmen, and Abandoned Lands, known as the Freedmen's Bureau. The Bureau, run by Major General Oliver Otis Howard, supervised relief efforts, furnishing clothing, medicine, and food to the freedmen as well as destitute whites. It also helped with the effort to create schools and churches and supplied legal support to help resolve conflicts over labor contracts and prevent fraud. Originally intended to also oversee leasing and sales of abandoned and confiscated property to the freedmen, the bureau provided land to only some thirty-five hundred blacks before being ordered to restore the property to its original owners. Preparing for the social revolution embedded in the transition from slavery to freedom would require much effort, but first the war had to be brought to a close.

On February 3, three Confederate commissioners—Vice President Alexander Stephens, John A. Campbell, a former Supreme Court justice, and R. M. T. Hunter, president of the Confederate Senate—boarded the *River Queen* at Hampton Roads and met with Lincoln and Seward. Peace balloons had been sent up previously, most notably when Horace Greeley met with Confederate agents at Niagara Falls in July 1864, but they had all popped for one reason or another: Lincoln insisted on the abandonment of slavery as a precondition, and Davis insisted on using the language of peace between "two countries." Lincoln had not seen his old friend Stephens for sixteen years. As the men talked, it became clear that they could not agree on terms, and as Lincoln reported to Congress, the conference "ended without result."[7]

A month later, on March 4, he was inaugurated for his second term. It rained all morning, but the sun shined through as Lincoln rose to speak. In a brief address, Lincoln offered his view of the origins of the war, never referring to the Confederates as anything but "insurgents." He acknowledged that "both parties deprecated war; but one of them would *make* war rather than let the nation survive; and the other would *accept* war rather than let it perish." He devoted much talk to God, noting that both sides "read the same Bible, and pray to the same God; and each invokes His aid against the other.... The prayers of both could not be answered; that of neither has been answered fully. The Almighty has His own purposes." Lincoln, whose generosity of spirit allowed him to forgive easily, concluded: "with malice toward none; with charity for all; with firmness in the right, as God gives us to see the right, let us strive to bind up the nation's wounds; to care for him who shall have borne the battle, and for his widow, and his orphan—to do all which may achieve and cherish a just, and a lasting peace, among ourselves, and with all nations."[8]

The military victories continued to come. Fort Fisher had fallen in January, giving the Union control of Wilmington, North Carolina, and cutting Lee's supply line. On April 2, after two days of battle that exacted more than ten thousand casualties combined (seven thousand of them Confederate), Lee ordered the evacuation of Petersburg and Richmond. On April 4, Lincoln visited Richmond with his son Tad. As he walked from the waterfront, thousands of blacks gathered in celebration. "I know I am free for I have seen Father Abraham and felt him," declared one woman. He made his way to the Confederate White House, where he sat in Jefferson Davis's study. He then went to the state house. A meeting with a small delegation of Confederates came to nothing, and he returned to Washington after a stop at army headquarters. On April 7, having heard of Sheridan's success, Lincoln wired to Grant: "Gen Sheridan says 'if the thing is pressed I think Lee will surrender.' Let the *thing* be pressed."[9]

After exchanging messages with Grant, on April 9, Robert E. Lee and his aide rode to Appomattox Courthouse to surrender. Lee had no choice. Any further combat would decimate the Army of Northern Virginia. And he refused to resort to a guerilla war that allowed swarms of his men to continue to fight a partisan battle on their own. The generals met around two o'clock in the afternoon at the home of Wilmer McLean, who ironically had moved there on fleeing Manassas after the first battle of Bull Run. Lee dressed in his finest uniform and wore a sword; Grant was muddy and had on a worn blouse as a coat. They discussed terms, and Grant generously offered not only to parole the army of twenty-eight thousand as long as men did not take up arms again but also to allow them to return home and keep their horses. An hour later, it was over. As news spread among the troops, cheers went up. "To have seen us," recalled one Union private, "no one would have supposed that for four long years we had been involved in a deadly war." "The war is over," Grant was reported to have said. "The rebels are our countrymen again, and the best sign of rejoicing after the victory will be to abstain from all demonstrations in the field." Grant provided rations for Lee's starving men, who had plenty of bullets left but no biscuits. By June, the other Confederate armies had surrendered and Jefferson Davis was in prison.[10]

Lincoln thought about how best to restore the union quickly. Retribution was not in his makeup. In what turned out to be his final speech, he signaled support for giving black men the right to vote. He continued to joust with radical congressmen in his own party, and he listened to the opinions of his cabinet members. He often recalled his dreams, and after meeting with Grant to hear a firsthand account of what transpired at Appomattox, he told of one in which he was in a vessel and "moving with great rapidity towards an indefinite shore." On April 14, Good Friday, in the afternoon before going to the theater, he took a carriage ride alone with his wife. He was joyous and cheerful. He told her, "I consider *this* day, the war, has come to a close."[11]

Despite being urged not to go out that evening, Lincoln assembled a party of four to see *Our American Cousin* at Ford's Theatre. Arriving late, he was resoundingly cheered as the orchestra played "Hail to the Chief." During the third act, John Wilkes Booth made his way to the presidential box. A prominent actor, the Maryland-born Booth supported the Confederacy and despised Lincoln as a tyrant and tool of the abolitionists. He was among the crowd on April 11 who had heard Lincoln endorse giving the vote to "very intelligent" blacks "and those who serve our cause as soldiers." "That means nigger citizenship," exclaimed Booth, swearing, "This is the last speech he will ever make." He contrived a plan to assassinate Lincoln, Johnson, and Seward, with the help of his henchmen, who had earlier plotted to kidnap the president and whisk him off to Richmond. The assault on Johnson miscarried; Lewis Powell repeatedly stabbed the bedridden Seward, but he survived; Booth shot the president in the head, leapt down to the stage and cried "Sic semper tyrannis"—"Thus always to tyrants." Lincoln was carried across the street and placed on a small bed in a narrow room. He lingered for nine hours, and then reached the indefinite shore of which he had dreamed.[12]

On April 16, Grant received a letter of condolence from Confederate general Richard Ewell. The officer wrote to assure Grant of Southern "feelings of unqualified abhorrence and indignation for the assassination of the President of the United States....No language can adequately express the shock produced upon myself, in common with all the other general officers confined here with me, by the occurrence of this appalling crime, and the seeming tendency in the public mind to connect the South and Southern men with it."[13]

"The public mind," in Ewell's apt phrase, knew not what to think, convulsed with sorrow in the North over the loss of Lincoln and in the South over the loss of the war. Shockingly, six weeks after the assassination, Andrew Johnson sought to implement his own restoration plan. Lincoln had first started thinking about reconstruction as early as 1863. His ideas developed over time and often collided with the markedly different ideas of radical Republicans. Little was settled except that the United States would be one and that slavery would be abolished. But under what terms would the states that had seceded regain their place? And how would Southern society navigate its journey from slave labor to free labor? Looking beyond a structural reconstruction of the nation, one Union officer confessed: "how are we to woo this people back to their old love for the Union is a mystery to me."[14]

Andrew Johnson wasted little time announcing his policies. With Congress out of session, he issued a proclamation that provided for amnesty and the restitution of property, except for slaves, to Southerners who took an oath of allegiance. The proclamation made exceptions of certain categories of Confederate officeholders and officers, as had Lincoln's proclamation, and added anyone owning more than $20,000 of taxable property. Johnson had risen from poverty, and he held deep animosity toward planter aristocrats. He was the only Southern senator to remain in the Union when secession came, and his activities as a pro-war Democrat and a military governor of Tennessee won him a spot on Lincoln's ticket. But like many Democrats, although he denied the legitimacy of secession, he supported states' rights generally. A former slaveholder, he also shared in the dominant racial ideology of his day.

Through the summer, under terms set by Johnson, constitutional conventions met and repudiated secession as well as the Confederate debt and ratified the Thirteenth Amendment, a condition for readmission. It was ratified on December 6 when Georgia approved it, the twenty-seventh out of thirty-six states to do so. And Johnson took great personal satisfaction from having thousands of members of the Southern elite come groveling for a special pardon.

Congress would not come into session until December. While some Republicans initially favored Johnson's lenient policies, radical Republicans such as Thaddeus Stevens were outraged by an approach that, in the end, would actually give the South additional congressional representation. Stevens sought the enfranchisement of blacks, an action opposed not only by Johnson but also by several Northern states, including Connecticut, which in the fall defeated a state amendment giving black men the vote.

On September 7, Thaddeus Stevens delivered a speech in Lancaster, Pennsylvania, in which he offered his views on the work of reconstruction, or restoration as Johnson preferred to call it. The duty of the government, Stevens proclaimed, was to punish the "rebel belligerents, and so weaken their hands that they can never again endanger the union." To help accomplish this he insisted that "the property of the chief rebels should be seized and appropriated to the payment of the national debt caused by the unjust and wicked war which they instigated." Stevens lambasted those who argued that since secession was unconstitutional the states had never actually left the Union and therefore they could not be treated as having forfeited their place. But then how, he wondered, might any reconstruction ever take place? "Reformation," he insisted, "*must* be effected; the foundation of their institutions both political, municipal, and social *must* be broken up and *relaid*, or all our blood and treasure have been spent in vain...the whole fabric of Southern society must be changed." The rebel states should be treated as conquered territories, de facto alien enemies, and the some seventy thousand "proud, bloated, and defiant rebels" should pay for what they had put the nation through.[15]

Johnson's "restoration" versus Stevens's "reformation" marked the grounds for the battles over reconstruction. Through the fall, under Johnson's terms, constitutional conventions gathered in Southern states, and these states held elections in anticipation of being quickly restored. But Congress had different ideas, and when the Thirty-ninth Congress began its work in December, members refused to seat Southern representatives. Instead, they created a joint committee to discuss reconstruction policy. The committee called witnesses and heard testimony about what was taking place on the ground in the former Confederacy. What they discovered would lead them to consider civil rights legislation and propose what would become the Fourteenth Amendment.

Republicans in Congress were especially alarmed at the reports of Southern actions directed at blacks. States such as Mississippi and South Carolina passed stringent codes that discriminated against the freedmen. These included vagrancy laws and annual employment contracts aimed at limiting the movements of blacks. The codes also forbade blacks from serving on juries, stipulated harsher punishments for crimes than those given to whites, and outlawed interracial marriage. The Freedman's Bureau was in a position to help protect blacks, but Johnson, in one of the first acts that would lead him into open warfare with Congress, on February 19, 1866, vetoed a bill to extend the life of the Bureau on the grounds that it was not constitutional. In July, Congress passed a new bill, over Johnson's veto, extending the life of the Bureau and creating Freedman's Courts to help protect black rights.

Johnson also vetoed a civil rights bill passed by Congress on March 13. The bill defined persons born in the United States as citizens and guaranteed them "full and equal benefit of all laws and proceedings for the Security of person and property." Even the bill's supporters recognized how transformative it was. By committing federal authorities to protecting the rights of its citizens, it redefined the role of the government. One senator, who supported the measure, admitted that "this species of legislation is absolutely revolutionary. But are we not in the midst of a revolution?"[16]

Not only was the bill passed over Johnson's veto; Congress, partly in response to the so-called black codes just mentioned, went about drafting and debating a new constitutional amendment, the Fourteenth, which would further protect civil rights. Section 1 defined all persons born in the United States as citizens and guaranteed them that no state law "shall abridge the privileges or immunities of citizens" or deprive any person of life, liberty, or property "without due process of law" or deny any person "equal protection of the laws." Section 2 set the terms for the apportionment of representation and, rather than give blacks the vote, simply reduced Southern representation. Section 3 prohibited anyone from holding office who had previously taken an oath to support the Constitution and then "engaged in insurrection or rebellion." Section 4 renounced the Confederate debt and confirmed the validity of the federal debt. On June 13, 1866, Congress submitted the amendment to the states. Every Republican in the House voted for it; every Democrat was opposed.

Abolitionists, who had been pressing for black suffrage, were keenly disappointed by section 2, which supported, implicitly at least, the rights of states to curtail voting on racial grounds. Thaddeus Stevens well understood that the amendment could not be everything he might have desired. Why do "I accept so imperfect a proposition?" he asked rhetorically. "I answer, because I live among men and not among angels."[17]

One congressional act Johnson did sign was the Southern Homestead Act. Enacted on June 21, it opened up forty-six million acres of public lands across the South (Alabama, Arkansas, Florida, Louisiana, Mississippi) to settlement and development. It differed from the Homestead Act of 1862 in that one could not purchase the land outright. The Act also made clear that blacks and whites were equally eligible. Oliver Howard expressed the optimism of many that this act would go a long way toward providing a solution to the problem of the transition from slavery to freedom. He said, "there is no reason why the poor whites and freedmen of the South cannot take advantage of the present homestead law, and enter a career of prosperity, that will secure them fortunes, elevate them socially and morally, and settle the many vexed issues that are now arising."[18]

It didn't turn out as Howard had hoped. Much of the land made available was of poor quality, and timber companies, through fraud, snatched up the premium acreage. The poor whites and blacks most in need of land were also the ones who did not have means to travel to the land or subsist while working it. Blacks also faced resistance from whites who feared losing a pool of wage laborers and did not want them to own their own property. A petition by a group trying to gain land in Florida asked Congress "to provide for our race such transportation, rations, building materials, tents, surgeons & surveyors and such legislation as will secure among ourselves honesty, industry and frugality and deliver us from the fear of all who maliciously hate and persecute us." Such material relief, however, was not forthcoming.[19]

The fall elections promised to serve as a referendum on presidential versus congressional reconstruction. Andrew Johnson took the unprecedented measure of embarking on a speaking tour to win support for his policy of reconciliation. Instead, he drove prospective conservative and moderate voters away with harangues that branded his opponents traitors and even suggested that providence had played a role in making him president. Race riots in Memphis in May and New Orleans in July gave the lie to Johnson's optimistic vision of a loyal South ready for readmission: the mob in New Orleans attacked delegates to a convention on black suffrage and murdered thirty-seven blacks. If anything, it seemed as if the embers of rebellion were about to reignite. Republicans dominated the election, both nationally and locally. Even in the Upper South, a new group of Unionists supportive of black civil rights gained power.

Legislators did not wait for the new members to be seated. On March 2, 1867, the Thirty-ninth Congress passed the First Reconstruction Act over Johnson's veto. The Act divided Confederate states into five military districts and made them subject to military authority, each commanded by a general. It also made state governments only provisional. When these states adopted a new constitution enfranchising black males and ratified the Fourteenth Amendment, they would then be readmitted. Johnson vetoed the Act as exceeding congressional authority. Congress also sought to check presidential autonomy by passing the Tenure of Office Act, which prevented Johnson from removing any executive branch officials whose appointment had required Senate confirmation.

It didn't take long before Johnson challenged this Act. On August 1, he suspended Edwin Stanton, the secretary of war, who supported congressional plans of reconstruction. Much to the chagrin of Republicans everywhere, Grant stepped in as interim secretary. He did so to support not Johnson but the military command in the South. Johnson removed several military commanders he thought too radical, including Philip Sheridan and Daniel Sickles. When the Senate refused to uphold Stanton's suspension, Grant vacated the office, and Stanton returned. On February 21, 1868, Johnson removed Stanton. Three days later, the House impeached him.

The trial began on March 30. Senator Charles Sumner supported conviction as "one of the great last battles with slavery.... Slavery has been our worst enemy, murdering our children, filling our homes with mourning, and darkening the land with tragedy; and now it rears its crest anew with Andrew Johnson as its representative." But other senators warned against setting a dangerous precedent such that one party with an overwhelming majority could oust the president if he was a member of the opposite party. Lyman Trumbull feared that "Blinded by partisan zeal, with such an example before them, they will not scruple to remove out of the way any obstacle to the accomplishment of their purposes, and what then becomes of the checks and balances of the constitution, so carefully devised and so vital to its perpetuity? They are all gone. In view of the consequences likely to flow from the day's proceedings, should they result in conviction on what my judgment tells me are insufficient charges and proofs, I tremble for the future of my country." In May, the Senate voted, and Johnson escaped conviction by one vote.[20]

By then, Republicans had realized that the current of public opinion was turning against them. Democrats had gained seats in state elections the previous year, carrying New York and Pennsylvania. And in Ohio and Minnesota, Democrats rallied to defeat ballot referendums for black male suffrage. Outside New England, black men in the North could not vote any more than freed slaves in the South.

On July 9, the Fourteenth Amendment was ratified, but it seemed that the promise of constitutional protection for all citizens only increased opposition and extralegal violence against some of them. New derogatory words entered the language: "scalawag" for Southerners who supported the Republicans and "carpetbagger" for Northerners who came south to help the freedmen. The Ku Klux Klan had been founded in Tennessee in June 1866, originally as a private social club, but it quickly morphed into an organization whose members were rabid opponents of Republican politics and black equality. Led by former Confederate officers, including Nathan Bedford Forrest, who had been responsible for the massacre at Fort Pillow and now served as "Grand Wizard" of the white-hooded secret society, the Klan claimed tens of thousands of members. Through the fall of 1868, they murdered white and black Republican leaders, terrorized the freedmen, and burned homes and schools. One journalist, touring the South after the war, observed: "the real question at issue in the South is not 'What shall be done with the negro?' but 'What shall be done with the white?'...The viciousness that could not overturn the nation is now mainly engaged in the effort to retain the substance of slavery. What are names if the thing itself remains?"[21]

During the presidential campaign of 1868, Thomas Nast, whose work for *Harper's Weekly* during and after the war helped sustain the cause of radical Republicans, offered one of his most searing indictments of the Democratic Party in his cartoon "This is a White Man's Government." Three men are standing on a prostrate black Union veteran. On the left, a caricature of the working-class Irishman whose handiwork at the Colored Orphan Asylum during the draft riots hangs in the background; in the middle, Nathan Bedford Forrest, whose belt buckle reads "CSA"

Thomas Nast, "This is a White Man's Government," *Harper's Weekly*, September 5, 1868. Courtesy of Library of Congress.

(Confederate States of America), his knife, "the lost cause," and medal "Ft. Pillow"; on the right is New York financier August Belmont waving money with which to buy votes. With the American flag and his Union cap lying at his side, the fallen man stretches toward the ballot box, just out of reach.

On accepting the Republican nomination for president, Grant closed with the words "Let Us Have Peace." His election victory over New York's Horatio Seymour showed a narrow margin in the total vote—3 million to 2.7—but a comfortable win with 53 percent of the vote and an Electoral College victory of 214 to 80. In eight states, however, the margin of difference in the popular vote was less than 5 percent. It was enough to make Republicans realize that though they had won the war, they might be losing the peace. Because they felt it was both right and politically expedient, Congress in February 1869 approved the Fifteenth Amendment, which stated that "the right of citizens of the United States to vote shall not be denied or abridged by the United States or by any State on account of race, color, or previous condition of servitude." Black men would be guaranteed the vote, and they would no doubt vote for the party of Lincoln. It was an astonishing accomplishment, whose rapidity left observers breathless. The radical abolitionist Parker Pillsbury observed that "suffrage for the negro is now what immediate emancipation was thirty years ago," and yet unlike emancipation it was achieved quickly.[22]

The Fifteenth Amendment became law in March 1870, but Grant's administration faced the problem of how to protect the expansion of the franchise against efforts by the Klan and others to keep voters from the polls. Congress in short order passed several Enforcement Acts, intended to prevent election fraud and "enforce the rights of citizens of the United States to vote in the several states of this union." They also passed the Ku Klux Klan Act, which sought to suppress the Klan's terrorist activities through arrests and prosecutions and authorized the president to suspend habeas corpus in areas of insurrection.

In many respects, 1870 marked the end of reconstruction. By that year, every state had been readmitted to the nation. In fact, all but three (Mississippi, Texas, and Virginia) had been readmitted by June 1868 (Georgia was admitted, then excluded again, and then readmitted in 1870 with the other states). By 1871, Congress had passed whatever legislation it was going to generate to support the freedmen and help reconstruct the South, and the Thirteenth, Fourteenth, and Fifteenth amendments were signed into law.

But if political reconstruction was over, economic reconstruction continued. It took the South decades to recover its output of cotton, rice, and sugar—in 1870 production stood at about two-thirds of that in 1860. Per capita income in the South continued to fall, from three-quarters to one-half the national average. Even though some individuals continued to have vast landholdings, the plantation as an economic center began to break down. The freedmen's initial response to emancipation was to assert autonomy by moving away from the master's house. Most blacks preferred small farms to plantations and quickly became embedded in various forms of land tenancy. They would often rent the land in return for cash or a share of their crop. These arrangements differed depending on what the landlord provided, and inevitably from season to season black farmers as well as white found they were always in debt, placing them in a cycle of always borrowing against future crops.

With slavery ended, there was a need for labor in the South, and a struggle ensued to make fair agreements between former planters, now landlords, and former slaves, now freedmen. Republican newspapers published letters reputed to be from ex-slaves negotiating for a fair deal. For example, Jourdon Anderson wrote to his former master, who wanted him to return to work for him:

> We have concluded to test your sincerity by asking you to send us our wages for the time we served you. This will make us forget and forgive old scores, and rely on your justice and friendship in the future. I served you faithfully for thirty-two years and Mandy twenty years. At $25 a month for me, and $2 a week for Mandy, our earnings would amount to $11,680. Add to this the interest for the time our wages has been kept back and deduct what you paid for our clothing and three doctor's visits to me, and pulling a tooth for Mandy, and the balance will show what we are in justice entitled to.... If you fail to pay us for faithful labors in the past we can have little faith in your promises in the future."[23]

In reality, few freedmen found fair deals. Indeed, they lost not only their economic but also their political independence as states passed assorted measures—literacy tests, residency requirements, poll taxes—aimed at keeping blacks from exercising the suffrage. One visitor to the South after the war offered a cogent analysis of the reasons for suppression. He said that white Southerners "admit" that the government has set the slaves free, but they "appear to believe that they still have the right to exercise over him the old control....They cannot understand the national intent as expressed in the Emancipation Proclamation and the Constitutional Amendment. I did not anywhere find a man who could see that the laws should be applicable to all persons alike; and hence even the best men hold that each State must have a negro code." Blacks, concluded one Southern lawyer, have "freedom in name, but not in fact."[24]

The most significant progress for freedmen came through educational efforts. Many Northerners flocked south to teach, and many Southern black institutions of learning emerged: Fisk (1866), Morehouse (1867), Hampton (1868). The use of federal and state funds, as well as private philanthropic contributions, produced a startling result: literacy among black teenagers rose from 10 percent in 1865 to over 50 percent by 1890. Schools of industrial labor, designed to provide training in mechanical arts and trades that would enable youth to earn a livelihood, were especially widespread. One such school, the Manassas Industrial School, opened on September 3, 1894. Frederick Douglass, celebrating on that day the fifty-sixth anniversary of his escape from slavery, delivered the dedication address and told the assembled crowd that "to found a school, in which to instruct, improve and develop all that is noblest and best in the souls of a deeply wronged and long neglected people, is especially noteworthy. This spot once the scene of fratricidal war, and the witness of its innumerable and indescribable horrors, is, we hope, hereafter to be the scene of brotherly kindness, charity and peace. We are to witness here, a display of the best elements of advanced civilization and good citizenship. It is to be a place where the children of a once enslaved people may realize the blessings of liberty and education, and learn how to make for themselves and for all others, the best of both worlds."[25]

But aside from tacit support of educational efforts, most Northerners had grown weary of the whole subject of reconstruction, seeking to heal what one writer called "the wounds and diseases of peace."[26] In 1872, the Amnesty Act restored officeholding rights to many former Confederates. In 1873, a financial panic seized America, and many politicians and activists turned their attention away from the problems of the South. With the election of 1874, Democrats gained control of the House. In 1875, the Supreme Court, in *United States v. Cruikshank*, ruled that only states, not individuals, were subject to federal prosecution for violating the constitutional rights of individuals. Since local authorities rarely tried to protect the freedmen, those who terrorized them could now act with impunity.

"Let us have done with Reconstruction," pleaded one New York news-paper in April 1870, "the country is tired and sick of it." From that point on, another phase, redemption—the restoring of conservative Democratic leadership to the states that had made up the Confederacy—proliferated. By 1875, nearly every state had shaken off Republican rule. The war had been over for ten years, and so, too, the desire to settle its outcome.[27]

By then, Mark Twain and Charles Dudley Warner had penned their summary statement about the tectonic shifts occasioned by the Civil War: The United States was saved, now singular and not plural, never again to be threatened seriously by disunion, though the tensions between state and nation in regard to the locus of authority would continue to resonate. Slavery was abolished, and the freedmen had obtained constitutional rights guaranteed to them by the federal government, though in most other ways their struggle to define the contours of freedom and achieve equality had only just begun. A powerful, centralized national government used the tools at hand to extend further a dynamic capitalistic ideology that would develop markets and commercial interests at home and abroad. Southern society was left devastated as wealth in property was entirely lost or devalued, cities were destroyed, shipping and rails were immobilized, livestock were slaughtered, and production was decimated. A generation of white males aged fifteen to thirty-nine participated in the war, and one out of three was left dead or wounded: With so much death (360,000 Union and 260,000 Confederate), romance, an ideal characteristic of the decades before the carnage, yielded to realism—a faith in facts and an understanding that life entailed an ongoing battle for survival.

The process of settling the conflict persisted well past 1875. Both sides continued to live with their memories of war, and both sides made use of it. Northerners would "wave the bloody shirt" to remind voters of the Union dead, and Southerners would craft a cult of "the lost cause," a belief that the Confederacy stood for a gallant and glorious endeavor. As new generations came of age, they couldn't possibly understand what the country had been through and what the soldiers had experienced. In July 1913, on the golden anniversary of the Battle of Gettysburg, thou-sands of white veterans, federal and rebel, walked the terrain again, gath-ered together, and reminisced. For both sides, the past would never end, and with the mist of nostalgia heavy in the air, they would seek to recap-ture and remake it.

Epilogue

Walt Whitman never met Lincoln, but he cherished him. Volunteering in Washington's hospitals during the war, he often caught a glimpse of the president. "I see the President almost every day," he wrote in 1863, "we have got so that we exchange bows, and very cordial ones." "I think well of the President," he confided another time. "He has a face like a hoosier Michael Angelo, so awful ugly it becomes beautiful, with its strange mouth, its deep cut, criss-cross lines, and its doughnut complexion." In June, he wrote to his mother: "I had a good view of the President last evening—he looks more careworn even than usual—his face with deep cut lines, seams, & his *complexion gray*, through very dark skin, a curious looking man, very sad." "Always to me," he observed, "a deep latent sadness in the expression."

Whitman praised Lincoln's leadership: "he has shown, I sometimes think, an almost supernatural tact in keeping the ship afloat at all, with head steady, not only not going down, and now certain not to, but with proud and resolute spirit, and flag flying in sight of the world, menacing and as ever." Another time he declared, "Mr. Lincoln has done as good as a human could do." "I think better of him," Whitman confessed, "than many do. He has conscience & homely shrewdness—conceals an enormous tenacity under his mild, gawky western manner."

The poet was in New York on the night Lincoln went to Ford's Theatre. Some fifteen years later, he was still trying to make sense of the assassination:

> The day, April 14, 1865, seems to have been a pleasant one throughout the whole land—the moral atmosphere pleasant too—the long storm, so dark, so fratricidal, full of blood and doubt and gloom, over and ended at last by the sun-rise of such an absolute

National victory, and utter break-down of Secessionism—we almost doubted our own senses! Lee had capitulated beneath the apple-tree of Appomattox. The other armies, the flanges of the revolt, swiftly follow'd. And could it really be, then? Out of all the affairs of this world of woe and failure and disorder, was there really come the confirm'd, unerring sign of plan, like a shaft of pure light—of rightful rule—of God?

In the immediate aftermath, Whitman wrote poems about Lincoln's death: "Hush'd Be the Camps Today," "When Lilacs Last in the Dooryard Bloom'd," "O Captain, My Captain." But it was with prose that he kept returning to the war, with prose that he tried to divine its meaning.

The war, he believed, was "not a struggle of two distinct and separate peoples, but a conflict (often happening, and very fierce) between the passions and paradoxes of one and the same identity—perhaps the only terms on which that identity could really become fused, homogenous, and lasting."

For Whitman, the war vindicated American democracy: "the movements of the late secession war, and their results, to any sense that studies well and comprehends them, show that popular democracy, whatever its faults and dangers, practically justifies itself beyond the proudest claims and wildest hopes of enthusiasts." "That our national democratic experiment, principle, and machinery, could triumphantly sustain such a shock," he believed, "is by far the most signal proof yet of the stability of that experiment, Democracy, and of those principles, and that Constitution." And that proof of democracy came "every bit as much from the south, as from the north.... I deliberately include all. Grand, common stock!" The "four years of lurid, bleeding, murky, murderous war" was volunteered for by "the People, of their own choice, fighting, dying for their own idea."

He kept returning to the soldiers, to the rank and file, to those remarkable specimens of American vitality, courage, and youth. During the war, he regularly visited wounded men, first in New York and then in Washington at the Armory Square Hospital. "I have been almost daily calling as a missionary," he wrote of his visits, "distributing now & then little sums of money—and regularly letter-paper and envelopes, oranges, tobacco, jellies, &c. &c."

In 1882, he published *Specimen Days,* a discursive series of entries, part memoir and part diary, primarily about his days during the war. He kept trying to find words to convey the stories of the sick and wounded, of the battle scenes, but words kept proving inadequate to experience: "what history, I say, can ever give—for who can know—the mad, determin'd tussle of the armies." "Of scenes like these, I say, who writes—whoe'er can write the story?"

But he continued writing until he could write no more, and then he tried to bid farewell:

> AND so good-bye to the war. I know not how it may have been, or may be, to others—to me the main interest I found, (and still, on recollection, find,) in the rank and file of the armies, both sides, and in those specimens amid the hospitals, and even the dead on the field. To me the points illustrating the latent personal character and eligibilities of these States, in the two or three millions of American young and middle-aged men, North and South, embodied in those armies—and especially the one-third or one-fourth of their number, stricken by wounds or disease at some time in the course of the contest—were of more significance even than the political interests involved. . . . Future years will never know the seething hell and the black infernal background of countless minor scenes and interiors, (not the official surface courteousness of the Generals, not the few great battles) of the Secession war; and it is best they should not—the real war will never get in the books. In the mushy influences of current times, too, the fervid atmosphere and typical events of those years are in danger of being totally forgotten. I have at night watch'd by the side of a sick man in the hospital, one who could not live many hours. I have seen his eyes flash and burn as he raised himself and recurr'd to the cruelties on his surrender'd brother, and mutilations of the corpse afterward. . . . Such was the war. It was not a quadrille in a ball-room. Its interior history will not only never be written—its practicality, minutiæ of deeds and passions, will never be even suggested. The actual soldier of 1862–'65, North and South, with all his ways, his incredible dauntlessness, habits, practices, tastes, language, his fierce friendship, his appetite, rankness, his superb strength and

animality, lawless gait, and a hundred unnamed lights and shades of camp, I say, will never be written—perhaps must not and should not be.

In 1888, a friend of Whitman asked him, "Do you go back to those days?"

"I do not need to," the poet responded. "I have never left them."[1]

NOTES

PREFACE

1. Karl Marx and Frederick Engels, "The American Civil War," *Die Presse*, March 26 and 27, 1862, www.marx.org/archive/marx/works/1862/03/26.htm.
2. Charles L. Brace, "The Key to Victory," *Independent*, August 22, 1861, 1.
3. Mark Twain, *The Gilded Age and Later Novels* (New York: Library of America, 2002), 134.

CHAPTER 1

1. *Charleston Mercury* quoted in James M. McPherson, *Ordeal by Fire: The Civil War and Reconstruction* (New York: Knopf, 1982), 129; Mississippi Declaration of Immediate Causes, in David and Jeanne Heidler, eds., *Encyclopedia of the American Civil War* (New York: W.W. Norton, 2000), 2244.
2. Cushing quoted in A. Leon Higginbotham, *In the Matter of Color: Race and the American Legal Process* (New York: Oxford University Press, 1980), 421; Ellsworth quoted in Paul Finkelman, *An Imperfect Union: Slavery, Federalism, and Comity* (Chapel Hill: University of North Carolina Press, 1981), 35; Jon Sensbach, " 'Self-Evident Truths' on Trial: African Americans in the American Revolution," in Andrew K. Frank, ed., *American Revolution: People and Perspectives* (ABC-CLIO), 43.
3. Thomas Jefferson, *Notes on the State of Virginia*, in Jefferson, *The Portable Thomas Jefferson*, ed. Merrill Peterson (New York: Penguin, 1977), 215.
4. Thomas Jefferson to James Madison, December 20, 1787, in Jefferson, *Portable Thomas Jefferson*, 430.
5. William Wirt Henry, *Patrick Henry: Life, Correspondence, and Speeches*, vol. 3 (New York: Scribner's, 1891), 549.
6. The texts of the Virginia and Kentucky Resolutions are available at the Avalon Project: Documents in Law, History, and Diplomacy, Yale Law School, http://avalon.law.yale.edu/18th_century/virres.asp.

7. Report of the Hartford Convention, January 15, 1815, U.S. Constitution online, www.usconstitution.net/hartford.html.

8. Thomas Jefferson to John Holmes, April 22, 1820, in Jefferson, *Portable Thomas Jefferson*, 568; Thomas Jefferson to William Short, April 13, 1820, Thomas Jefferson Papers, ser. 1, Correspondence, 1651–1827, Library of Congress, http://memory.loc.gov/cgi-bin/ampage?collId=mtj1&fileName= mtj1page051.db&recNum=1223.

9. David Walker's *Appeal,* available at the Web site Documenting the American South, http://docsouth.unc.edu/nc/walker/menu.html; William Lloyd Garrison quoted in Louis P. Masur, *1831: Year of Eclipse* (New York: Hill and Wang, 2001), 29.

10. James Gholson quoted in Masur, *1831,* 55.

11. John C. Calhoun, Speech on Reception of Abolition Petitions, February 6, 1837, in *The Works of John C. Calhoun.* vol. 2 (New York: D. Appleton, 1888), 631.

12. Hammond quoted in James M. McPherson, *Battle Cry of Freedom: The Civil War Era* (New York: Oxford University Press, 1988), 100.

13. Tocqueville quoted in Masur, *1831,* 152; Adams quoted, 160.

14. Jackson quoted in Masur, *1831,* 168.

15. Emerson quoted in McPherson, *Battle Cry of Freedom,* 51.

16. *Speech of Hon. Langdon Cheves in the Southern Convention, at Nashville, Tennessee, November 14, 1850* (Nashville: Southern Rights Association, 1850), 30.

17. Abraham Lincoln, "Eulogy on Henry Clay, July 6, 1852," in *The Collected Works of Abraham Lincoln,* ed. Roy P. Basler (New Brunswick: Rutgers University Press, 1953) (*CW*), 2:130.

18. *Appeal of the Independent Democrats* quoted in McPherson, *Ordeal by Fire,* 88.

19. Lincoln, "Speech on the Kansas-Nebraska Act, October 16, 1854," in *CW*, 2:255.

20. *Independent* quoted in McPherson, *Ordeal by Fire,* 101; Lincoln, "House Divided" Speech at Springfield, Illinois, June 16, 1858, in *CW*, 2:467.

21. Emerson quoted in McPherson, *Battle Cry of Freedom,* 209.

22. *Richmond Enquirer* and *Richmond Whig* quoted in McPherson, *Battle Cry of Freedom,* 211.

23. *Atlanta Confederacy* quoted in Richard H. Sewell, *A House Divided: Sectionalism and Civil War, 1848–1865* (Baltimore: Johns Hopkins University Press, 1988), 76.

24. Abraham Lincoln to Alexander H. Stephens, December 22, 1860 in *CW*, 4:160.

25. Seward quoted in McPherson, *Battle Cry of Freedom,* 198.

CHAPTER 2

1. Jefferson Davis, Inaugural Address as Provisional President, February 18, 1861, in *Jefferson Davis: The Essential Writings,* ed. William J. Cooper, Jr. (New York: Modern Library, 2004), 200.

2. Alexander Stephens, "Cornerstone Speech, March 21, 1861," in Jon Wakelyn, ed., *Southern Pamphlets on Secession, November 1860–April 1861* (Chapel Hill: University of North Carolina Press, 1996), 406.

3. Abraham Lincoln, "Speech to Germans at Cincinnati," February 12, 1861, and "Speech at Independence Hall, Philadelphia," February 22, 1861, in *The Collected Works of Abraham Lincoln*, ed. Roy P. Basler (New Brunswick: Rutgers University Press, 1953) (*CW*), 4:203, 240–41.

4. Abraham Lincoln, "First Inaugural Address," March 4, 1861, in *CW*, 4:262–71.

5. Toombs quoted in James M. McPherson, *Ordeal by Fire: The Civil War and Reconstruction* (New York: Knopf, 1982), 145.

6. Lee quoted in James M. McPherson, *Battle Cry of Freedom: The Civil War Era* (New York: Oxford University Press, 1988), 281.

7. James McPherson points out that "a campaigning army of 100,000 men … required 2,500 supply wagons and at least 35,000 animals, and consumed 600 tons of supplies each day." *Battle Cry of Freedom*, 325.

8. Wilma King, ed., *Tryphena Blanch Holder Fox, A Northern Woman in the Plantation South* (Columbia: University of South Carolina Press, 1993), 130.

9. Jefferson Davis to Theophilus H. Holmes, December 21, 1862 in Davis, *Jefferson Davis*, 275; Winfield Scott to George McClellan, May 3, 1861, Civil War Biographies, www.civilwarhome.com/scottmcclellananaconda.htm.

10. Abraham Lincoln, "Message to Congress in Special Session, July 4, 1861," in *CW*, 4:431, 433.

11. P. Burns to Ann Maceubbin, June 10, 1861, in Andrew Carroll, ed., *War Letters* (New York: Washington Square Press, 2001), 49.

12. Both sides organized their armies in similar fashion. A company consisted of one hundred men, a regiment consisted of ten companies, a brigade consisted of four regiments, a division consisted of three brigades, and a corps usually consisted of three divisions.

13. James Horrocks, *My Dear Parents: An Englishman's Letters Home from the American Civil War*, ed. A. S. Lewis (London: Golancz, 1982), 80.

14. Henry Adams to Charles Francis Adams, Jr., August 5, 1861, in Louis P. Masur, ed., *"The Real War Will Never Get in the Books": Selections from Writers during the Civil War* (New York: Oxford University Press, 1993), 5; McClellan quoted in McPherson, *Battle Cry of Freedom*, 359; 364.

15. "The War in Missouri," *New York Times*, September 8, 1861, 1.

16. Abraham Lincoln to John C. Fremont, September 11, 1862, in *CW*, 4:518.

17. Charles L. Brace, "The Key to Victory," *Independent*, August 22, 1861, 1; Frederick Douglass quoted in McPherson, *Ordeal by Fire*, 266.

18. Howard Jones, *Union in Peril: The Crisis over British Intervention in the Civil War* (Chapel Hill: University of North Carolina Press, 1992), 84.

19. Jefferson Davis, "Message to Confederate Congress, November 18, 1861," in Davis, *Jefferson Davis*, 218.

20. Abraham Lincoln, "Annual Message to Congress, December 3, 1861," in *CW*, 5:36, 49.

Chapter 3

1. Meigs quoted in David Herbert Donald, *Lincoln* (New York: Simon and Schuster, 1995), 330.

2. Quoted in Jean Smith, *Grant* (New York: Simon and Schuster, 2001), 300.

3. Editorial quoted in Smith, *Grant*, 164; Henry Adams to Charles Francis Adams, Jr., March 15, 1862, in Louis P. Masur, ed., *"The Real War Will Never Get in the Books": Selections from Writers during the Civil War* (New York: Oxford University Press, 1993), 6; Jefferson Davis, "Inaugural Address," in *Jefferson Davis: The Essential Writings,* ed. William J. Cooper, Jr. (New York: Modern Library, 2004), 227.

4. Quoted in James M. McPherson, *Battle Cry of Freedom: The Civil War Era* (New York: Oxford University Press, 1988), 414.

5. Stephen W. Sears, ed., *For Country, Cause and Leader: The Civil War Journal of Charles B. Haydon* (New York: Ticknor and Fields, 1993), 171; Ulysses S. Grant, *Personal Memoirs of Ulysses S. Grant* (New York: Cosimo Classics, 2007), 185; Confederate soldier quoted in James M. McPherson, *Ordeal by Fire: The Civil War and Reconstruction* (New York: Knopf, 1982), 229; Herman Melville, "Shiloh," in *Battle Pieces* (New York: BiblioLife, 2009), 47.

6. James Milner quoted in Theodore Karamanski, *Rally 'round the Flag: Chicago and the Civil War* (New York: Rowman and Littlefield, 2006), 91.

7. Milner quoted in Karamanski, *Rally 'round the Flag,* 90.

8. Quoted in James M. McPherson, *For Cause and Comrades* (New York: Oxford University Press, 1997), 118.

9. W. Joseph Bray, Jr., and Jerome J. Hale, eds., *Letters to Lauretta, 1849–1863,* quoted in Garold L. Cole, ed., *Civil War Eyewitnesses: An Annotated Bibliography of Books and Articles 1986–1996* (Columbia: University of South Carolina Press, 2000), 141.

10. Julia A. Drake, ed., *The Mail Goes Through; Or, the Civil War Letters of George Drake,* in Garold L. Cole, ed., *Civil War Eyewitnesses: An Annotated Bibliography of Book and Articles, 1955–1986* (Columbia: University of South Carolina Press, 1988), 37; Stephen Sears, ed., *For Country, Cause and Leader: The Civil War Journal of Charles B. Haydon* (New York: Ticknor and Fields, 1993), 300.

11. Kathleen Davis, ed., *Such Are the Trials: The Civil War Diaries of Jacob Gantz* (Ames: Iowa State University Press, 1991), 69; Stephen W. Sears, *Journal of Charles B. Haydon,* 263; Alvin Burnett quoted in Gerald L. Cole, ed., *Civil War Eyewitnesses* (Columbia: University of South Carolina Press, 2000), 18; Michael Taylor, ed., *The Cry Is War, War, War: The Civil War Correspondence of Lts. Burwell Thomas Cotton and George Job Huntley* (Dayton, Ohio: Morningside House, 1994), 77; Henry Graves quoted in Bell Irvin Wiley, *The Life of Johnny Reb*

(Baton Rouge: Louisiana University Press, 1979), 35; Kenneth Noe, ed., *A Southern Boy in Blue: The Memoir of Marcus Woodcock* (Knoxville: University of Tennessee Press, 1996), 139.

12. Sears, *Journal of Charles B. Haydon,* 234, 249; Barry Popchock, ed., *Soldier Boy: The Civil War Letters of Charles O' Musser* (Iowa City: University of Iowa Press, 1995), 213; David D. Bard, quoted in Cole, *Civil War Eyewitnesses,* 2:11.

13. Benjamin Freeman quoted in "The American Civil War: Conscription," Civil War Talk, www.etymonline.com/cw/conscript.htm.

14. David Heidler and Jeanne Heidler, eds., *Encyclopedia of the American Civil War* (New York: Norton, 2000), 295.

15. Abraham Lincoln to George McClellan, April 9, 1862, in *The Collected Works of Abraham Lincoln,* ed. Roy P. Basler (New Brunswick: Rutgers University Press, 1953) (*CW*), 5:184–85.

16. Samuel Emsinger, *Letters to Lanah: A Series of Civil War Letters,* in Cole, *Civil War Eyewitnesses,* 33; quoted in Gary Gallagher, *The Confederate War* (Cambridge, Mass.: Harvard University Press, 1997), 88.

17. Daniel H. Hill quoted in Grady McWhiney and Perry Jamieson, *Attack and Die: Civil War Military Tactics and the Southern Heritage* (Tuscaloosa: University of Alabama Press, 1984), 4.

18. Fitzhugh Lee, *General Lee: A Biography of Robert E. Lee* (1894; reprint, Cambridge, Mass.: DaCapo Press, 1994), 171.

19. McClellan to Abraham Lincoln, July 7, 1862, in Abraham Lincoln Papers, Library of Congress, http://memory.loc.gov/cgi-bin/query/P?mal:3:./temp/~ammem_nF2i::.

20. Lincoln quoted in David Herbert Donald, *Lincoln* (New York: Random House, 1995), 359.

21. Abraham Lincoln, "Message to Congress," March 6, 1862, in *CW,* 5:145.

22. Charles Sumner, "Ransom of Slaves at the National Capital," Speech in the Senate, March 31, 1862, in *The Works of Charles Sumner,* vol. 6 (Boston: Lee and Shephard, 1874), 438.

23. Lincoln quoted in Donald, *Lincoln,* 363.

24. *Letters of a Family during the War for the Union, 1861–1865* (privately printed, n.d.), 2:442; Abraham Lincoln, "Appeal to Border States Representatives for Compensated Emancipation, July 12, 1862," *CW,* 5:317–19.

25. Lincoln quoted in James M. McPherson, *This Mighty Scourge: Perspectives on the Civil War* (New York: Oxford University Press, 2007), 219.

26. Horace Greeley, "The Prayer of Twenty Millions," *New York Tribune,* August 16, 1862, in Heidler and Heidler, *Encyclopedia of the American Civil War,* 2426.

27. Abraham Lincoln to Horace Greeley, August 22, 1862, in *CW,* 5:388.

28. Frederick Douglass, *Douglass' Monthly,* September 1862.

29. Quoted in James M. McPherson, *Crossroads of Freedom* (New York: Oxford University Press, 2002), 85, 86; Edward Bates quoted in Donald, *Lincoln,* 372.

30. Lee to Jefferson Davis, September 3, 1862, Son of the South, www.sonofthesouth.net/leefoundation/LettersJeffersonDavis.htm; William Child to his wife, n.d., in Andrew Carroll, ed., *War Letters* (New York: Washington Square Press, 2001), 76.

31. Abraham Lincoln, "Address on Colonization," in *CW*, 5:372; Chase quoted in James M. McPherson, *Tried by War: Abraham Lincoln as Commander in Chief* (New York: Penguin Press, 2008), 129. Also see Eric Foner, "Lincoln and Colonization," in Foner, ed., *Our Lincoln: New Perspectives on Lincoln and His World* (New York: Norton, 2008), 135–66.

32. Sumner and Greeley quoted in John Hope Franklin, *The Emancipation Proclamation* (New York: Anchor Books, 1965), 58–59; Charles Fessenden Morse, *Letters Written during the Civil War, 1861–1865* (1898), 224. Abraham Lincoln to Hannibal Hamlin, September 28, 1862, in *CW*, 5:444.

33. Seymour quoted in Allen C. Guelzo, *Lincoln's Emancipation Proclamation: The End of Slavery in America* (New York: Simon and Schuster, 2004), 211.

34. Quoted in Franklin, *Emancipation Proclamation*, 64–65; Jefferson Davis, Message to Confederate Congress, January 12, 1863, in Davis, *Jefferson Davis*, 290.

35. "Dead at Antietam," *New York Times*, October 20, 1862.

36. Heidler and Heidler, *Encyclopedia of the American Civil War*, 778.

37. Jefferson Davis, "Speech in Jackson, Mississippi, December 26, 1862," in Davis, *Jefferson Davis*, 278–79.

38. Abraham Lincoln, Message to Congress, December 1, 1862 in *CW*, 5:537.

39. Ralph Waldo Emerson, "The President's Proclamation," *Atlantic Monthly* 10 (November 1862): 642.

CHAPTER 4

1. Louis P. Masur, ed., *"The Real War Will Never Get in the Books": Selections from Writers during the Civil War* (New York: Oxford University Press, 1993), 192–93.

2. Allen C. Guelzo, *Lincoln's Emancipation Proclamation: The End of Slavery in America* (New York: Simon and Schuster, 2004), 292–95.

3. Jefferson Davis, "Message to Confederate Congress," January 12, 1863, in *Jefferson Davis: The Essential Writings*, ed. William J. Cooper, Jr. (New York: Modern Library, 2004), 290; William Smith, March 17, 1863, in Ira Berlin et al., *Free at Last: A Documentary History of Slavery, Freedom, and the Civil War* (New York: New Press, 1992), 99; Alexander Caldwell, January 11, 1863, quoted in James M. McPherson, *For Cause and Comrades* (New York: Oxford University Press, 1997), 121; Maria Randall Allen, ed., *My Darling Wife: The Letters of Washington George Nugent*, quoted in Garold L. Cole, *Civil War Eyewitnesses: An Annotated Bibliography of Books and Articles, 1986–1996* (Columbia: University of South Carolina Press, 2000), 69; Abraham Lincoln to

John A. McClernand, January 8, 1863, in *The Collected Works of Abraham Lincoln*, ed. Roy P. Basler (New Brunswick: Rutgers University Press, 1953) (*CW*), 6:8.

4. Abraham Lincoln to Joseph Hooker, January 26, 1863, in *CW*, 6:78–79.

5. Lincoln quoted in David Herbert Donald, *Lincoln* (New York: Simon and Schuster, 1995), 436.

6. Clement Vallandigham, "The Great Civil War in America," in *Speeches, Arguments, Addresses and Letters of Clement Vallandigham* (New York: J. Walter, 1864), 418–53.

7. Abraham Lincoln to Erastus Corning and Others, June 12, 1863, in *CW*, 6:260–69; quoted in McPherson, *For Cause and Comrades*, 145.

8. Lincoln quoted in Donald, *Lincoln*, 445.

9. "The Invasion of the North," *Harper's Weekly*, June 27, 1863, 402.

10. Quoted in Donald, *Lincoln*, 440.

11. A. P. Carpenter, letter, July 30, 1863, Southern Methodist University, www2.smumn.edu/deptpages/~history/civil_war/companyk.htm.

12. Theodore Reichardt, *Diary of Battery A, First Regiment Rhode Island Light Artillery* (Providence: N. Bangs Williams, 1865), 96.

13. Michael Fellman, *The Making of Robert E. Lee* (Baltimore: Johns Hopkins University Press, 2003) 154.

14. Samuel Cormany, July 5, 1863, in James Mohr, ed., *The Cormany Diaries: A Northern Family in the Civil War* (Pittsburgh: University of Pittsburgh Press, 1982), 326.

15. Abraham Lincoln to George C. Meade, July 14, 1863, in *CW*, 6:327–28.

16. Petition quoted in James M. McPherson, *Ordeal by Fire: The Civil War and Reconstruction* (New York: Knopf, 1982), 332–33.

17. Davis quoted in James M. McPherson, *Atlas of the Civil War* (New York: Running Press, 2005), 91; Jefferson Davis to Robert Johnson, July 14, 1863, in Davis, *Jefferson Davis*, 304.

18. Howard K. Beale, ed., *Diary of Gideon Welles* (New York: Norton, 1960), 1:365; Jean Edward Smith, *Grant* (New York: Simon and Schuster, 2001), 287; Sherman quoted in B. H. Liddell Hart, *Sherman: Soldier, Realist, American* (Cambridge, Mass.: DaCapo Press, 1993), 197.

19. Testimony from Victims of New York Draft Riots, July 1863, American Social History Project, http://historymatters.gmu.edu/d/6216.

20. Quoted in Donald, *Lincoln*, 431.

21. Douglass quoted in Guelzo, *Lincoln's Emancipation Proclamation*, 247.

22. *New York Independent* quoted in "Letters," *New York Times Book Review*, October 4, 2009, 6; "A Typical Negro," *Harper's Weekly*, July 4, 1863, 429.

23. Charles Henry Gooding to Abraham Lincoln, September 28, 1863, in Virginia M. Adams, ed., *On the Altar of Freedom: A Black Soldier's Civil War Letters from the Front* (New York: Warner Books, 1992), 119.

24. Michael Freyburger, *Gold Rush and Civil War Letters,* quoted in Cole, *Civil War Eyewitnesses,* 34; Robert Garth Scott, ed., *Fallen Leaves: The Civil War Letters of Major Henry Livermore Abbott* (Kent: Ohio State University Press, 1991), 199; quoted in McPherson, *For Cause and Comrades,* 127; Grant quoted in McPherson, *Battle Cry of Freedom,* 687n.

25. Abraham Lincoln to James C. Conkling, August 26, 1863, in *CW,* 6:406–10.

26. Quoted in Donald, *Lincoln,* 457.

27. Quoted in McPherson, *Battle Cry of Freedom,* 681; Henry Adams to Charles Francis Adams, Jr., October 2, 1863, in Masur, ed., *"Real War,"* 14.

28. John S. Roper, "Letter Written during Battle of Missionary Ridge," November 23, 1863, *Journal of the Illinois State Historical Society* 6 (April 1913): 504.

29. Quoted in Donald, *Lincoln,* 466.

30. Stephen W. Sears, ed., *For Country, Cause and Leader: The Civil War Journal of Charles B. Haydon* (New York: Ticknor and Fields, 1993), 242.

CHAPTER 5

1. Stephen W. Sears, ed., *For Country, Cause and Leader: The Civil War Journal of Charles B. Haydon* (New York: Ticknor and Fields, 1993), 221; quoted in William C. Davis, *Look Away: History of the Confederate States of America* (New York: Free Press, 2002), 246.

2. Davis, *Look Away,* 246.

3. George W. Bagby quoted in Emory Thomas, *The Confederate Nation, 1861–1865* (New York: Harper and Row, 1979), 142.

4. Sarah Woolfolk Wiggins, ed., *The Journals of Josiah Gorgas,* 1857–1878 (Tuscaloosa: University of Alabama Press, 1995), 43; Robert E. Lee to Jefferson Davis, March 25, 1864, Son of the South, www.sonofthesouth.net/leefoundation/LettersJeffersonDavis3.htm.

5. Quoted in John Allan Wyeth, *That Devil Forrest: Life of General Nathan Bedford Forrest* (Baton Rouge: Louisiana State University Press, 1989), 333; Michael Freyburger, *Gold Rush and Civil War Letters,* quoted in Garold L. Cole, ed., *Civil War Eyewitnesses: An Annotated Bibliography of Books and Articles, 1986–1996* (Columbia: University of South Carolina Press, 2000), 36.

6. James H. Dennison, *Dennison's Andersonville Diary* (Kankakee, Ill.: Kankakee County Historical Society, 1987), 61.

7. Quoted in Jean Edward Smith, *Grant* (New York: Simon and Schuster, 2001), 349.

8. Gary W. Gallagher, *The Spotsylvania Campaign* (Chapel Hill: University of North Carolina Press, 1998), 113.

9. Martha Derby Perry, comp., *Letters from a Surgeon of the Civil War* (Boston: Little, Brown, 1906), 208–9.

10. David Herbert Donald, *Lincoln* (New York: Simon and Schuster, 1995), 506.

11. David Heidler and Jeanne Heidler, eds., *Encyclopedia of the American Civil War* (New York: Norton, 2000), 2373.

12. Quoted in James M. McPherson, *This Mighty Scourge* (New York: Oxford University Press, 2007), 171; Greeley quoted in James M. McPherson, *Battle Cry of Freedom: The Civil War Era* (New York: Oxford University Press, 1988), 762; Charles Francis Adams, *Richard Henry Dana: A Biography* (Boston: Houghton Mifflin, 1890), 264–65; Donald, *Lincoln*, 517; Abraham Lincoln, Memorandum, August 23, 1864, in *The Collected Works of Abraham Lincoln*, ed. Roy P. Basler (New Brunswick: Rutgers University Press, 1953) (*CW*), 7:514.

13. Stephen Sears, ed., *The Civil War Papers of George B. McClellan* (Cambridge, Mass.: DaCapo Press, 1992), 595.

14. *Gerrit Smith on McClellan's Nomination and Acceptance* (New York: Loyal Publication Society, 1864), 10.

15. Oliver Willcox Norton, *Army Letters, 1861–1865* (n.p.: privately printed, 1903), 101.

16. *Encyclopedia of the American Civil War*, 145; William M. Anderson, ed., *We Are Sherman's Men: The Letters of Henry Orendorff* (Macomb: Western Illinois University, 1986), 115.

17. Charles Bracelen Flood, *1864: Lincoln at the Gates of History* (New York: Simon and Schuster, 2009), 280; Strong quoted in McPherson, *Battle Cry of Freedom*, 773.

18. Planter quoted in McPherson, *Battle Cry of Freedom*, 775; quoted in Albert E. Castel, *Decision in the West: Atlanta Campaign of 1864* (Topeka: University of Kansas Press, 1992), 546.

19. Sheridan quoted in James M. McPherson, *Tried by War: Abraham Lincoln as Commander in Chief* (New York: Penguin Press, 2008), 245–46; C. Vann Woodward, ed., *Mary Chesnut's Civil War* (New Haven: Yale University Press, 1982), 648.

20. Olynthus B. Clark, ed., *Downing's Civil War Diary* (Des Moines: Historical Department, 1916), 227.

21. Abraham Lincoln, Response to Serenade, November 10, 1864, in *CW*, 8:101.

22. Strong quoted in Donald, *Lincoln*, 546; Sergeant quoted in William C. Davis, *Lincoln's Men* (New York: Free Press, 1999), 225; Adams quoted in John C. Waugh, *Reelecting Lincoln: The Battle for the 1864 Presidency* (Cambridge, Mass.: DaCapo Press, 2001), 357.

23. *Examiner* in Waugh, *Reelecting Lincoln*, 358; Grant in Waugh, *Reelecting Lincoln*, 360; Lee quoted in Joseph T. Glatthaar, *General Lee's Army: From Victory to Collapse* (New York: Free Press, 2008), 408.

24. Sherman quoted in McPherson, *This Mighty Scourge*, 121.

25. Quoted in Mark Grimsley, *The Hard Hand of War* (Cambridge: Cambridge University Press, 2008), 169.

26. Abraham Lincoln to William T. Sherman, December 26, 1864, in *CW*, 8:181.

27. Sherman quoted in B. H. Liddell Hart, *Sherman: Soldier, Realist, American* (Cambridge, Mass.: DaCapo Press, 1993), 358.

28. Jefferson Davis, Message to Confederate Congress, May 2, 1864, in *Jefferson Davis: The Essential Writings*, ed. William J. Cooper, Jr. (New York: Modern Library, 2004), 336.

Chapter 6

1. Robert E. Lee to Andrew Hunter, January 11, 1865, Son of the South, www.sonofthesouth.net/leefoundation/LettersAndrewHunter.htm.

2. Cobb quoted in James M. McPherson, *Ordeal by Fire: The Civil War and Reconstruction* (New York: Knopf, 1982), 77.

3. Virginia Ingraham Burr, ed., *The Secret Eye: The Journal of Ella Gertrude Clanton Thomas, 1848–1889* (Chapel Hill: University of North Carolina Press, 1990), 236; 243.

4. Thomas W. Cutrer, ed., *Longstreet's Aide: The Civil War Letters of Major Thomas J. Goree* (Charlottesville: University Press of Virginia, 1995), 137.

5. David Herbert Donald, *Lincoln* (New York: Simon and Schuster, 1995), 554.

6. William T. Sherman, Special Order Number 15, January 16, 1865, Freedmen and Southern Society Project, www.history.umd.edu/Freedmen/sfo15.htm.

7. Donald, *Lincoln*, 559.

8. Abraham Lincoln, "Second Inaugural Address," March 4, 1865, in *The Collected Works of Abraham Lincoln*, ed. Roy P. Basler (New Brunswick: Rutgers University Press, 1953) (*CW*), 8:332–33.

9. Quoted in Edna Greene Medford, "Imagined Promises, Bitter Realities," in Harold Holzer et al., *The Emancipation Proclamation* (Baton Rouge: Louisiana State University Press, 2006), 35; Donald, *Lincoln*, 580.

10. Herman J. Viola, ed., *The Memoirs of Charles Henry Veil* (New York: Orion Books, 1993), 66; Jean Edward Smith, Grant (New York: Simon and Schuster, 2001), 406.

11. Donald, *Lincoln*, 592–93.

12. Donald, *Lincoln*, 588.

13. Richard Ewell to U. S. Grant, April 16, 1865, in David Heidler and Jeanne Heidler, eds., *Encyclopedia of the American Civil War* (New York: Norton, 2000), 2386.

14. Kenneth P. McCutchan, ed., *Dearest Lizzie: The Civil War as Seen through the Eyes of Lieutenant Colonel James Maynard Shanklin* (Evansville, Ind.: Willard Library Press, 1988), 191.

15. *Speech of the Honorable Thaddeus Stevens, Delivered in the City of Lancaster, September 7th, 1865* (Lancaster, Pa.: Examiner and Herald, 1865), 1–8.

16. Quoted in Eric Foner, *Reconstruction: America's Unfinished Revolution, 1863–1877* (New York: Harper and Row, 1988), 245.

17. Foner, *Reconstruction*, 255.

18. Howard quoted in Michael L. Lanza, "'One of the Most Appreciated Labors of the Bureau': The Freedman's Bureau and the Southern Homestead Act," in Paul Cimbala and Randall Miller, eds., *The Freedman's Bureau and Reconstruction* (New York: Fordham University Press, 1999), 70.

19. Quoted in Lanza, " 'One of the Most Appreciated Labors,' " 80.

20. *Proceedings of the Trial of Andrew Johnson* (Washington, D.C.: Rives and Bailey, 1868), 958; Horace White, *The Life of Lyman Trumbull* (New York: BiblioLife, 2008), 319.

21. Sidney Andrews, *The South since the War* (Boston: Ticknor and Fields, 1866), 224–25.

22. Parker Pillsbury to Susan B. Anthony, in Ida Husted Harper, *The Life and Work of Susan B. Anthony* (Indianapolis: Bobbs-Merrill, 1898), 1:246.

23. Leon Litwack, *Been in the Storm So Long: The Aftermath of Slavery* (New York: Vintage, 1980), 334.

24. Andrews, *South since the War*, 398; 370.

25. "Speech at the Dedication of the Manassas Industrial School," Frederick Douglass Papers, Library of Congress, http://memory.loc.gov/cgi-bin/query/P?mfd:1:./temp/~ammem_Du1o::.

26. Walt Whitman, "Origins of Attempted Secession," in *Complete Prose Works* (New York: Library of America, 1982), 997.

27. Quoted in James M. McPherson, *Ordeal by Fire: The Civil War and Reconstruction* (New York: Knopf, 1982), 546.

Epilogue

1. Walt Whitman to Nathaniel Bloom and John F. S. Gray, March 19, 1863; Walt Whitman to Louisa Van Velsor Whitman, June 30, 1863; Walt Whitman to James P. Kirkwood, [April 27], 1864, all in Edwin Haviland Miller, ed., *The Correspondence of Walt Whitman*, vol. 1, *1842–1867* (New York: New York University Press, 1961), 83; 113; 213; *Specimen Days* and "Death of Abraham Lincoln," in *Walt Whitman: Complete Poetry and Collected Prose* (New York: Library of America, 1982), 732–33; 778–79; 1040. On the general subject of writers and the Civil War see Edmund Wilson, *Patriotic Gore: Studies in the Literature of the American Civil War* (New York: Farrar, Straus, and Giroux, 1963); Daniel Aaron, *The Unwritten War: American Writers and the Civil War* (New York: Oxford University Press, 1973); and Louis P. Masur, ed., *"The Real War Will Never Get in the Books": Selections from Writers during the Civil War* (New York: Oxford University Press, 1993).

FURTHER READING

The literature on the Civil War era is vast. The best single volume covering its overall history is James M. McPherson, *Battle Cry of Freedom: The Civil War Era*. I have omitted from this list the scores of superb military histories of specific campaigns and battles. Readers interested in military history might profitably consult the work of Peter Cozzens, William C. Davis, Gary Gallagher, Gordon Rhea, Stephen Sears, and Jeffrey Wert, to name a few prolific authors. The official records published by the War Department are *The War of the Rebellion: A Compilation of the Official Records of the Union and Confederate Armies (1889–1901)* and are available in print, on CD-Rom, and online at Cornell University's Web site The Making of America: http://digital.library.cornell.edu/m/moawar/waro.html.

Blight, David. *Race and Reunion: The Civil War in American Memory*. Cambridge, Mass.: Harvard University Press, 2002.

Boritt, Gabor, ed. *Why the Confederacy Lost*. New York: Oxford University Press, 1993.

Burlingame, Michael. *Abraham Lincoln: A Life*. Baltimore: Johns Hopkins University Press, 2008.

Cooper, William J. *Jefferson Davis, American*. New York: Vintage, 2001.

Davis, William C. *Look Away: History of the Confederate States of America*. New York: Free Press, 2002.

Donald, David. *Lincoln*. New York: Simon and Schuster, 1995.

Eaton, Clement. *A History of the Southern Confederacy*. New York: Free Press, 1965.

Faust, Drew Gilpin. *Mothers of Invention: Women of the Slaveholding South in the American Civil War*. Chapel Hill: University of North Carolina Press, 2004.

————. *This Republic of Suffering: Death and the American Civil War*. New York: Knopf, 2008.

Flood, Charles Bracelen. *1864: Lincoln at the Gates of History*. New York: Simon and Schuster, 2009.

Foner, Eric. *Reconstruction: America's Unfinished Revolution, 1863–1877*. New York: Harper and Row, 1988.

Foote, Shelby. *The Civil War: A Narrative*. 3 vols. New York: Vintage, 1986.

Franklin, John Hope. *Reconstruction after the Civil War*. Chicago: University of Chicago Press, 1961. Reprint, 1994.

Freehling, William W. *The Road to Disunion*. Vol. 1. *Secessionists at Bay, 1776–1854*. New York: Oxford University Press, 1990.

———. *The Road to Disunion*. Vol. 2. *Secessionists Triumphant, 1854–1861*. New York: Oxford University Press, 2007.

Gallagher, Gary W. *The Confederate War*. Cambridge, Mass.: Harvard University Press, 1997.

Glatthar, Joseph T. *Forged in Battle: The Civil War Alliance of Black Soldiers and White Officers*. Baton Rouge: Louisiana State University Press, 2000.

———. *General Lee's Army: From Victory to Collapse*. New York: Free Press, 2009.

Goodwin, Doris Kearns. *Team of Rivals: The Political Genius of Abraham Lincoln*. New York: Simon and Schuster, 2006.

Grimsley, Mark. *The Hard Hand of War*. Cambridge: Cambridge University Press, 1995.

Guelzo, Allen C. *Lincoln's Emancipation Proclamation: The End of Slavery in America*. New York: Simon and Schuster, 2004.

Heidler, David, and Jeanne Heidler, eds. *Encyclopedia of the American Civil War*. New York: Norton, 2000.

Holzer, Harold. *Lincoln President-Elect: Abraham Lincoln and the Great Secession War, 1860–1861*. New York: Simon and Schuster, 2008.

Howe, Daniel Walker. *What Hath God Wrought: The Transformation of America, 1815–1848*. New York: Oxford University Press, 2007.

Levine, Bruce. *Confederate Emancipation: Southern Plans to Free and Arm Slaves during the Civil War*. New York: Oxford University Press, 2006.

Litwack, Leon. *Been in the Storm So Long: The Aftermath of Slavery*. New York: Vintage, 1980.

Manning, Chandra. *When This Cruel War Is Over: Soldiers, Slavery, and the Civil War*. New York: Vintage, 2008.

Masur, Louis P. *1831: Year of Eclipse*. New York: Hill and Wang, 2001.

McPherson, James M. *Battle Cry of Freedom: The Civil War Era*. New York: Oxford University Press, 1988.

———. *Crossroads of Freedom*. New York: Oxford University Press, 2002.

———. *For Cause and Comrades*. New York: Oxford University Press, 1997.

———. *Ordeal by Fire: The Civil War and Reconstruction*. New York: Knopf, 1982.

———. *This Mighty Scourge: Perspectives on the Civil War*. New York: Oxford University Press, 2007.

———. *Tried by War: Abraham Lincoln as Commander in Chief*. New York: Penguin Press, 2008.

McWhiney, Grady, and Perry Jamieson. *Attack and Die: Civil War Military Tactics and the Southern Heritage*. Tuscaloosa: University of Alabama Press, 1984.

Mitchell, Reid. *Civil War Soldiers*. New York: Vintage, 1997.

Nelson, Scott, and Carol Sheriff. *A People at War: Civilians and Soldiers in America's Civil War, 1854–1877*. New York: Oxford University Press, 2008.

Oakes, James. *The Radical and the Republican: Frederick Douglass, Abraham Lincoln and the Triumph of Antislavery Politics*. New York: Norton, 2007.

Paludan, Phillip Shaw. *"A People's Contest": The Union and Civil War, 1861–1865*. New York: Harper and Row, 1988.

Potter, David. *The Impending Crisis, 1848–1861*. New York: Harper and Row, 1976.

Richardson, Heather Cox. *West from Appomattox: The Reconstruction of America after the Civil War*. New Haven, Conn.: Yale University Press, 2008.

Royster, Charles. *The Destructive War: William Tecumseh Sherman, Stonewall Jackson and the Americans*. New York: Vintage, 1993.

Stampp, Kenneth. *The Era of Reconstruction, 1865–1877*. New York: Vintage, 1967.

———. *The Peculiar Institution: Slavery in the Ante-Bellum South*. Reprint, New York: Vintage, 1989.

Thomas, Emory. *The Confederate Nation, 1861–1865*. New York: Harper and Row, 1979.

Varon, Elizabeth R. *Disunion: The Coming of the American Civil War, 1789–1859*. Chapel Hill: University of North Carolina Press, 2008.

Wilentz, Sean. *The Rise of American Democracy*. New York: Norton, 2005.

Wiley, Bell Irvin. *The Life of Billy Yank: The Common Soldier of the Union*. Baton Rouge: Louisiana State University Press, 1979.

———. *The Life of Johnny Reb: The Common Soldier of the Confederacy*. Updated ed. Baton Rouge: Louisiana State University Press, 2007.

INDEX